Richard Anthony Proctor

The Spectroscope and it's Work

Richard Anthony Proctor

The Spectroscope and it's Work

ISBN/EAN: 9783744688963

Printed in Europe, USA, Canada, Australia, Japan

Cover: Foto ©ninafisch / pixelio.de

More available books at **www.hansebooks.com**

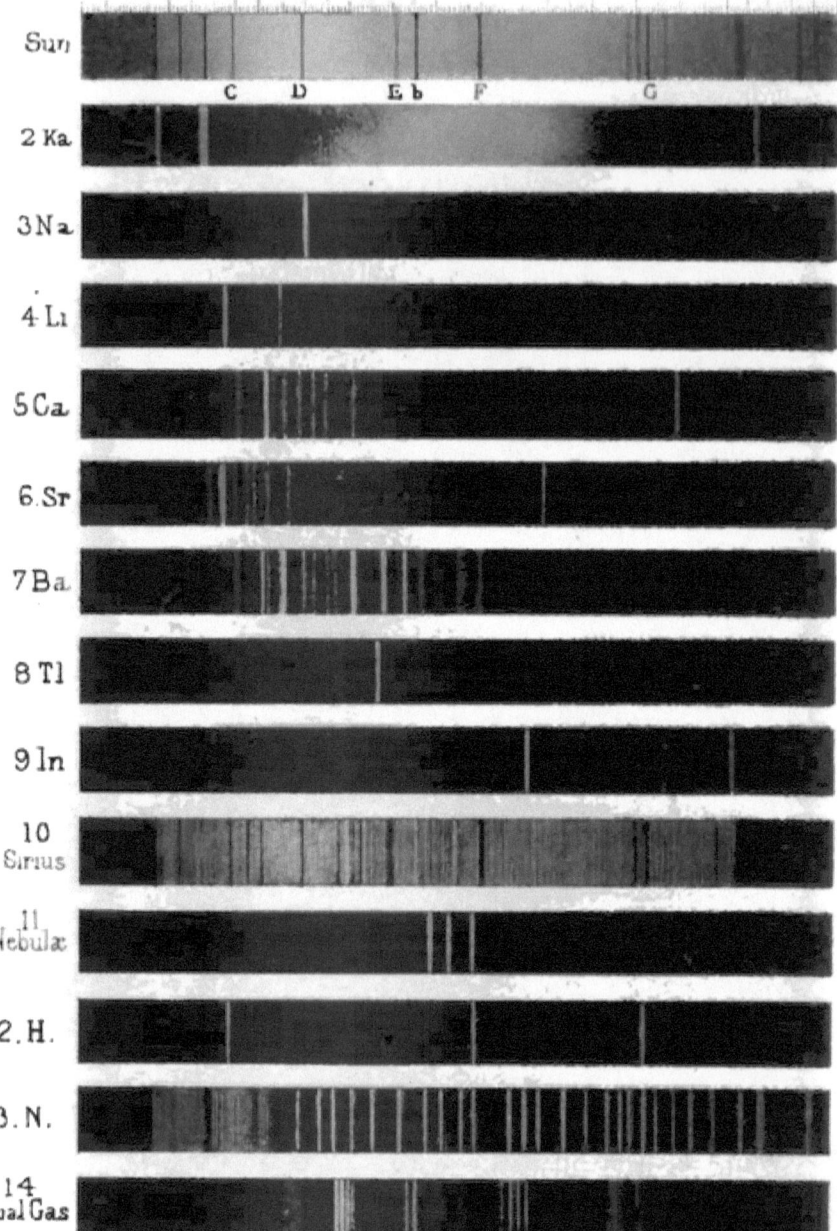

MANUALS OF ELEMENTARY SCIENCE.

THE
SPECTROSCOPE
AND ITS WORK.

BY

RICHARD A. PROCTOR,

*Author of "Saturn and its System," "The Sun," "The Moon,"
"The Universe," &c., &c.*

PUBLISHED UNDER THE DIRECTION OF
THE COMMITTEE OF GENERAL LITERATURE AND EDUCATION,
APPOINTED BY THE SOCIETY FOR PROMOTING
CHRISTIAN KNOWLEDGE.

LONDON:
SOCIETY FOR PROMOTING CHRISTIAN KNOWLEDGE,
NORTHUMBERLAND AVENUE, CHARING CROSS, W.C.;
43, QUEEN VICTORIA STREET, E.C.;
26, ST. GEORGE'S PLACE, HYDE PARK CORNER, S.W.
BRIGHTON: 135, NORTH STREET.
NEW YORK: E. & J. B. YOUNG & CO.

1885.

PREFACE.

I HAVE endeavoured to make this little treatise on Spectroscopic Analysis clear and simple for beginners, but at the same time accurate, and as complete as possible within so limited a space—following, in this respect, the plan already adopted in my elementary treatises on Astronomy and Physical Geography. In order to make room for subjects properly belonging to Spectroscopy, several subjects which are very fully treated of in large works on the Spectroscope (and indeed in one not containing more letterpress than the present) have been dealt with very briefly. It seems to me that—to mention but one such subject—full accounts of the various contrivances for obtaining intense heat and light, such as that with which Schellen occupies the first fifty-two pages of his treatise on Spectrum Analysis, are unsuitable even for large works intended for the general student, and are altogether out of place in an elementary treatise, necessarily limited in size. I doubt, indeed, whether anything can be usefully said in textbooks respecting details of the construction of instruments which the observer (who alone could profit by such explanations) must possess and employ. A few minutes devoted to the examination of the instrument itself will, in such a case, be of more use than many hours' study of textbook explanations.

On the other hand, I have endeavoured to give a full account of all the principles on which the application of Spectroscopy depends, as also of all the chief methods of observation and their results.

I am greatly indebted to Mr. J. BROWNING, the eminent optician, for the use of many cuts illustrating various forms of Spectroscopes, and their adjuncts.

CONTENTS.

CHAPTER I.
ANALYSIS OF LIGHT—THE SOLAR SYSTEM.

Spectroscopic Analysis Defined, p. 5—Refrangibility of Light, ib.—Reflection of Light, 6—Refraction of Light, 7—Rays which cannot be Reflected, 8—Experiment, ib.—Refraction through a Medium, 9—The Prism, 10—Refraction through a Prism, 11—First Case, ib.—Second Case, 12—Third Case, ib.—Prismatic Dispersion of Light, 13—The Solar Spectrum, 14—Dispersion of Coloured Light, 15.

CHAPTER II.
DARK SPACES IN THE SPECTRUM.

Wollaston's Observations, p. 16—Shape of Aperture, 17—Fraunhofer's Lines, 18—Angle of Minimum Deviation, 21—Collimating Lens, 22—The Spectroscope, 23—Spectroscopic Batteries, 24—Direct Vision Prism, 32—Direct Vision Spectroscopes, 33—Compound Prisms, 34—Half Prisms, 35—Measuring the Spectrum, 36.

CHAPTER III.
VARIOUS ORDERS OF SPECTRA.

Spectra of Solid and Liquid Bodies, p. 39—Heat Rays and Chemical Rays, 40—Spectrum of Glowing Vapours, 43—Bunsen's Burner, 44—The Electric Lamp, ib.—Various Vapour Spectra, 46—Various Orders of Vapour Spectra, 48—Spectrum of Reflected Light, 49—Absorption Spectra, 50—The Micro-spectroscope, 51—Absorption Spectra of Fluids, 52—Spectrum of Blood, 53—Spectrum of Aqueous Vapour, 54.

CHAPTER IV.
INTERPRETATION OF THE SOLAR SPECTRUM.

Researches of Kirchhoff and Bunsen, p. 55—Kirchhoff Interprets Solar Dark Lines, 57—The Solar Sodium Lines, 58—Iron Lines, 60—Constituent Vapours of the Sun's Atmosphere, 62—Interpretation of Various Spectra, 64—Spectroscopic Analysis of the Sun's Surface, 66—Spectrum of Sunspots, 67.

CHAPTER V.
THE SOLAR PROMINENCES, CORONA, ETC.

Spectroscopic Study of Solar Prominences, p. 70—The Prominence Spectrum, 72—The Sierra Spectrum, 73—Huggins's Method of Observing Prominences, 74—Results, 76—The Real Solar Atmosphere, 78—The Solar Corona, 79—Its Spectrum, 80—The Spectrum of the Zodiacal Light, 82.

CHAPTER VI.
SPECTRA OF THE STARS, MOON, PLANETS, COMETS, ETC.

Star Spectra, p. 83—The Star Spectroscope, 84—Measuring Lines in Star Spectra, 87—Spectra of Aldebaran and Betelgeux, 88—Spectrum of Sirius, 89—Various Orders of Star Spectra, ib.—Spectra of New Stars, 92—Of Star Clusters and Nebulæ, 94—Gaseous Nebulæ, 96—Spectra of Comets, 97—Winnecke's Comet, 98—Coggia's Comet, 99—Spectra of Meteors, ib.—Spectrum of the Moon, 102—Of Venus and Mars, ib.—Of Jupiter and Saturn, 103—Of Uranus and Neptune, 104.

CHAPTER VII.
ATMOSPHERIC LINES IN THE SOLAR SPECTRUM.

The Spectrum of the Atmosphere, p. 104—Of Aqueous Vapour, 105—Of Lightning, 106—Of the Aurora Borealis, 107.

CHAPTER VIII.
MEASURING MOTIONS OF RECESSION AND APPROACH.

Waves of Coloured Light, p. 110—Effect of Motion on Wave-length of Light, 112—Recession and approach of Stars, 114—Of Prominence Matter, etc., 117—Movements in the Solar Atmosphere, 118—Uprush and Downrush in the Sun's Atmosphere, 120—Solar Explosions, 121—Study of the Sun's Rotation and of the Motions of Planets by the Spectroscopic Method, 125.

ADDENDA.

Photographs of Spectra, p. 128—Bright line Spectra of Nebulæ, ib.—Spectrum of Meteorites, ib.—The two forms of Comet Spectra, ib.

THE SPECTROSCOPE AND ITS WORK.

CHAPTER I.

ANALYSIS OF LIGHT—THE SOLAR SYSTEM.

The spectroscope is an instrument for analysing light. By its means the rays of various colours forming a beam of white light are sifted so as to be separately discernible by their effects ; coloured light, when compound, is analysed into such component colours as by their combination make up its observed tint ; light really of a single colour is shown to be such, and its true colour exactly determined. But the spectroscope has other and more important uses. For by its means we can ascertain the elementary structure of bodies shining with particular tints simple or compound, and the nature of bodies which, being only partially transparent, absorb particular colours ; while the condition of such bodies, as to heat, pressure, motion, &c., can, in certain cases, be determined. In fine, spectroscopic analysis—that is, research carried on with the spectroscope—affords a means of solving many questions respecting the structure and condition of bodies terrestrial and celestial, and respecting most delicate problems of chemical and microscopical investigation, which had appeared altogether inscrutable before this method of research had been invented.

The property of light on which spectroscopic analysis principally depends is what is called refrangibility, or the quality by which light, when in its course it passes from one transparent medium into another of different structure or density, has the direction of its path more or less altered. Rays of different colour being differently affected when thus deflected, or *refracted*, as it is called, can be separated from each other by submitting them to suitable processes of refraction. What, then, we have first to do, rightly to understand the work of the spectroscope, is to examine the nature and laws of the refraction of light, and to distinguish refraction from other processes which light may undergo.

When light falls on an opaque polished surface, the rays are reflected according to a simple law. Thus, if the ray R I (fig. 1) fall on the polished surface A B at I, it will be reflected on the course I S, such that the angle R I Q, between I R and the perpendicular I Q, is equal to the angle S I Q between I S and the same perpendicular. So that if A S R B be a semicircle, having I as centre, the arc A S is equal to the arc B R. A fraction of the light falling on A B, however, illuminates this surface and makes it visible, some of the rays being irregularly reflected from the various particles composing the surface. The less polished the surface the greater will be the proportion of rays thus scattered to those regularly reflected.

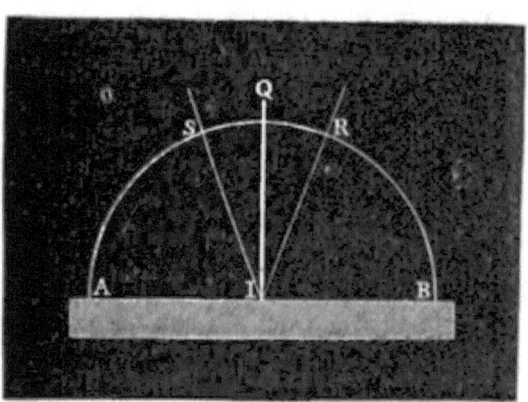

Fig. 1.—Illustrating the law of the reflection of light.

A portion of the light is also absorbed by the surface, the proportion of the rays thus absorbed depending on the nature of the surface. The surface also may absorb more rays of some colours than of others, and thus the rays by which it is seen will not be proportioned in the same way, as to colour, as those falling on the surface. It is this power of absorbing more or less of different coloured rays which gives to different surfaces their various colours.

If the substance on which the light falls is not opaque, but more or less transparent, then while a portion of the rays falling on the surface are regularly reflected, another portion scattered, and some also absorbed, a considerable portion are refracted through the transparent substance, passing onwards through it in straight lines as before, but no longer in the direction in which they were before travelling. Thus let the ray R I (fig. 2), passing through one transparent medium, as air, fall upon another transparent but denser medium, as water, at I, and let Q I P be perpendicular to the common surface of both media. Then the portion not reflected at I will not travel onwards along the prolongation of R I,

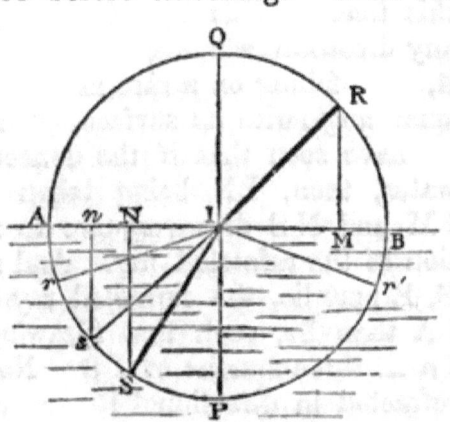

Fig. 2.—Illustrating the total reflection of rays at the surface of water.

but be bent into such a path as I S, the angle S I P being less than the angle R I Q. If, on the other hand, S I be a ray passing through a transparent medium, and at I falling on the surface of another transparent medium of less density, then the portion not reflected at I will pass into the rarer medium, not on its former course, but on such a path as I R, the angle R I Q being greater than the angle S I P. And although this deviation due to refraction does not follow a constant law for all substances, like the deviation due to reflection, yet there is a constant law for the refraction of light from one to another of two given transparent media. Thus, let the path R I (fig. 2) be in dry air of given density and heat, and I S in distilled water of given heat; draw a circle, Q A S, about I as centre, and R M, S N, square to A B; then whatever the direction of R I, the ratio of N I to M I remains constant, being nearly as three to four for the substances named. For other two substances the ratio would still be constant for all directions of R I, but the ratio would not be the same as for air and water.

If a ray proceeding on the path R I in a rarer medium is refracted into the path I S in a denser, then a ray proceeding on the path S I in the denser will be refracted into the path I R in the rarer medium. It follows from this that whereas rays falling on a denser medium in any direction whatever will be partly refracted through it, rays falling on a rare medium, so as to make a very small angle with its surface, will not be refracted. Thus we have seen that if the denser medium A P B is of water, then, I N being taken equal three-fourths of I M and N S drawn square to A B, I S is the direction of the refracted ray. And no matter how close to B, R may lie, the refracted ray can never lie closer to I A than I s, such that (drawing s n square to A B) I n = three-fourths of I B. Now the ray S I will be refracted in direction I R, and a ray in any direction between P I and s I will be refracted into the air between the directions I Q and I B; but a ray to I from any direction between s I and A I manifestly cannot be refracted according to the law described. It is found that in such cases the light is entirely reflected by the surface A I B, so that a ray as r I is reflected in direction I r'. For such rays, the surface A B acts the part of a perfect mirror.

All these properties can be tested by experiment. Thus, if r S P (fig. 2) be the bottom of a basin of water, a mark at S will be seen by an eye at R, as though the mark were at x, for the rays from S will reach the eye in the direction I R. Again, an eye under water at S will see an object at R in the direction S I. An eye under water at r (fig. 3), and directed towards the part of the surface lying beyond I to the right in the figure, will not see any object placed as R above that surface, but will see an object placed as r' below the surface. It will be the same if the eye at r is outside a glass vessel containing the water. Thus, if A P B be a glass bowl containing small fish, an eye at r outside the bowl will see in direction r I the reflected image of a fish at r', which fish will also be visible nearly in its true place by rays proceeding directly from r' to r. Accordingly, the fish and its image in the mirror-like surface of the water (viewed from below) will be seen, just as we may see at the same time a person himself and his image in a mirror.

It is clearly seen that the effect of refraction must be to separate rays of different kind which had been travelling in one direction, if such rays are differently affected by refraction. And in order to effect this, we should only have to allow the rays after refraction, as at I (fig. 2), to travel each on its new course far enough to get them as widely separated as we required, were it not for the fact that light is absorbed in passing through glass, water, or whatever other medium we employ; and before a sufficient separation had been effected, no visible light would remain for us to observe.

If we take a transparent medium, as glass, bounded by parallel sides, as M M' (fig. 3), an incident ray, F R, will be refracted at R in the direction R I, and on reaching I will be again refracted in the direction I S parallel to R F; for since a ray proceeding in direction I R would follow the course

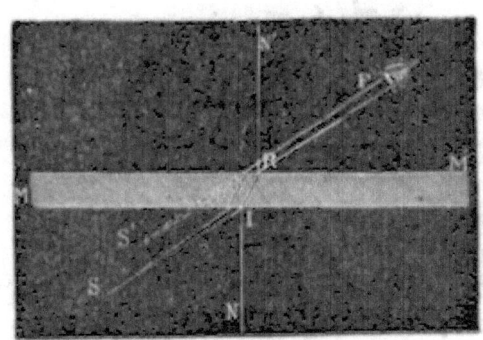

Fig. 3.—Illustrating the refraction of light through a medium bounded by parallel faces.

R F, making with the perpendicular R N' the angle F R N', the ray R I which makes with the surface at I the same angle which I R makes with the surface at R, must be refracted into a course I S, making with the perpendicular I N the same angle S I N. Here again, then, we fail to separate rays of light which falling together at R may be differently refracted; for though during the portion R I of their course they are diverging, they become parallel at I, and separate therefore no farther from each other.

But if the surface at I be not parallel to the surface at R, there will no longer be this parallelism; the separated rays will continue to diverge, and we shall have made one step at least towards the analysis of light. It was such reasoning as this which led Grimaldi, and later, Newton, to employ media bounded by non-parallel planes in their experimental researches on light.

We are thus introduced to the use of triangular prisms for the analysis of light. A prism is a wedge-shaped figure (fig. 4). It is defined by Euclid as a solid figure bounded by five surfaces, two of which (A B C and *a b c*) are triangles, equal, similar, and parallel to each other, while the other three (A *b*, *b* C, and C *a*) are rectangles.

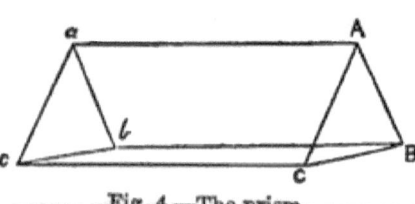

Fig. 4.—The prism.

Of these surfaces the triangular need not concern us *as surfaces;* they might be incomplete and unpolished, or they might be wholly or partly changed. So long as the rectangular portions are perfect as surfaces, at least where the light passes through them, the action of the prism will not be impaired. Moreover, in most uses of prisms for analysing light two of the rectangular faces only are employed. The glass drops of a chandelier are convenient instances of prismatic figures.

Fig. 5 illustrates the manner in which the prism acts on light which is refracted in passing through it. A B C represents a section of the prism parallel to its triangular faces. The ray D*e* falling on A B at *e* is bent *towards* the prolongation of the perpendicular *f e* in direction *e h*. At *h* it is again bent *from* the perpendicular *h g* in direction *h* E. The deviation from D D′, the original course of the light rays, is in this case increased at *h*, the total deflection being the angle between E *h*, produced, and D D′. Here A B and A C are the two rectangular faces of the prism

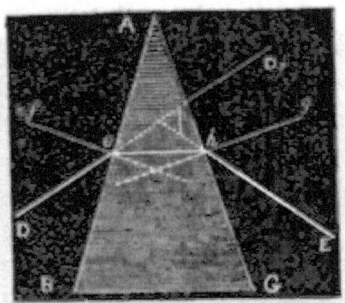

Fig. 5.—Path of a ray through a prism.

called into action. The edge A between these faces is called the *refracting edge;* the angle between them is called the *refracting angle;* and the divergence of the ray after emergence at *h* from the course it had before incidence at *e* is called the *angle of deviation.*

The first general case of deviation is illustrated in fig. 6. Here the incident ray S I is refracted in direction I E, or *from* the refracting edge, and in emerging at E is again refracted in direction E R, or *from* the refracting edge, the angle of deviation being the *sum* of the two deviations. When the deviations are equal we have the special case pictured in fig. 5.* In fig. 7

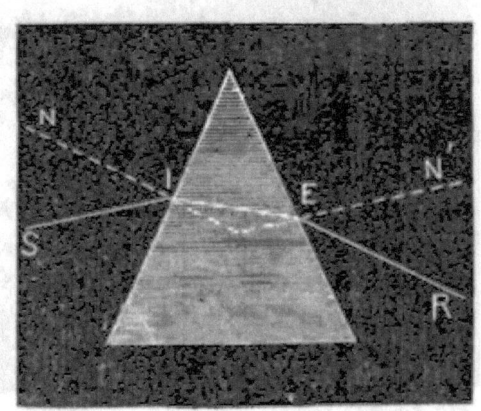

Fig. 6.—The first general case of refraction through a prism.

---

* By a singular mistake the cases illustrated in figs. 6 and 7 with the special case pictured in fig. 5 are dealt with in Schellen as the three general cases, the general case illustrated in fig. 8 being entirely omitted. In the English edition the mistake is left uncorrected, and it has been reproduced in elementary treatises on the spectroscope.

the second general case is illustrated. Here the incident ray being perpendicular to the surface at I undergoes no refraction, but passes on in the straight line S I E. On emerging at E it undergoes refraction *from* the refracting edge, and the angle of deviation is the angle between S E produced and E R. Thus we have in this case the same kind of deviation as the former, that is, deviation *from* the refracting edges both at incidence and emergence, but the deviation produced at one place only,—at emergence or at incidence according to the course pursued. The third general case

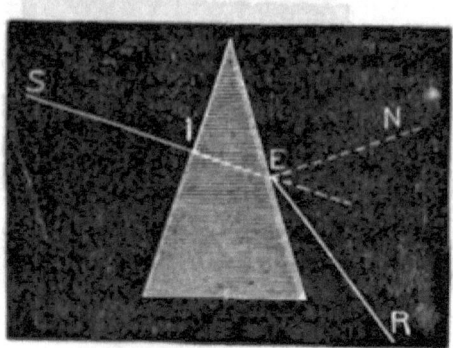

Fig. 7.—The second general case of refraction through a prism.

is illustrated in fig. 8, where we see the incident ray S I deflected towards the refracting edge at I, but *from* it when emerging at E, in direction E R, the angle of deviation being the excess of the second deviation over the first. As the path S I E R

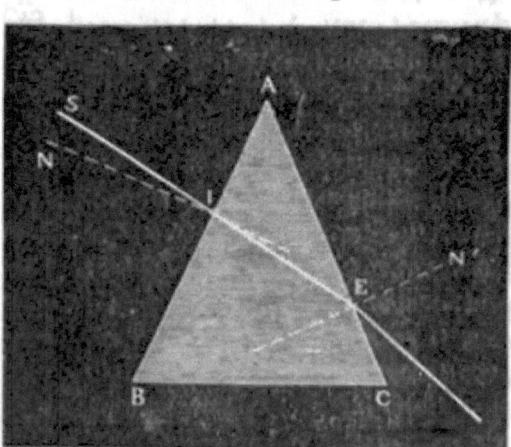

Fig. 8.—The third general case of refraction through a prism.

may be followed either in the direction S I E R or in the direction R E I S, all possible cases of refraction through a prism are illustrated in the figs. 6, 7 and 8. We see that in all cases deviation is *from* the refracting edge of the prism; for in the two first there is only deviation from the edge; and though in the third case there is deviation at I towards the edge, it is manifest that the deviation *from* the edge at E is much greater.* In every case then the action of the prism causes a deviation *from* the refracting edge.

The prism, therefore, possesses the property required for the separation of rays of light, if they are not all refracted in the same way when passing from one medium into another (or, technically, if they are not all of the same refrangibility). For in that case rays from the same source of light, having different directions when they emerge from the prism, will continue to separate more and more from each other. Thus, let A B (fig. 9) represent a beam of sunlight passing

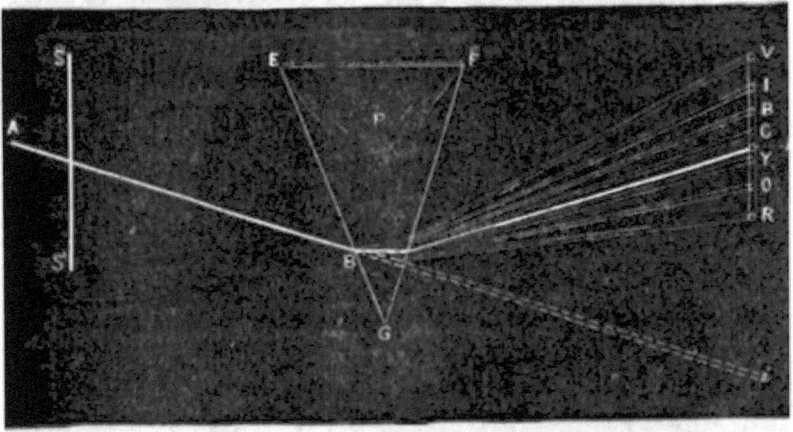

Fig. 9.—Illustrating the action of a prism on rays of different coloured light.

through a circular aperture in a screen S S', P a prism of glass, and at V R let there be a surface on which the rays of light may fall. If the prism P were removed, the rays would pass to *i*, and form there a small oval image of the circular opening in the screen S S'. The prism being interposed, the rays will be refracted in the

* Because the interior angle A E I is less than the exterior angle E I B. It is easily seen from fig. 2, and the matter explaining it, that the greater the angle between S I and the surface the less will be the divergence of the ray at I from its original course S I.

manner already described. If they are all of the same kind, they will all be refracted in the same degree, and the beam of light will only be bent, as shown by the bent bright line A B i' in fig. 9, and will form a small oval white image at i'. But if the rays forming the beam are unequally refrangible, some will be more bent, proceeding after emergence to V, or I, or B, others less, proceeding to R, or O, or Y; and the light which otherwise would have been gathered at i' will be spread along some such strip as V G R. Newton found (as Grimaldi had before noticed, however) that this happens when sunlight is refracted by a prism, and that the rays which thus differ in refrangibility differ in colour also, the rays which are most refracted being violet, those least refracted being red, the colours corresponding to intermediate degrees of refrangibility being, in order (after violet), indigo, blue, green, yellow, and orange. In other words, this experiment showed that sunlight consists of rays of seven different colours—violet, indigo, blue, green, yellow, orange, and red—these rays being less and less refrangible in this order. The streak of coloured light thus formed by the action of the prism is called the *prismatic spectrum;* the violet end of the spectrum contains the most refracted part of the light, while the red end contains the part least refracted; and the rays towards the violet end are commonly called *the more refrangible rays*, those towards the red end being called *the less refrangible rays*. This way of speaking should be carefully noted.

If rays of any one colour of the seven were all equally refrangible, we should find in the experiment illustrated by fig. 9 that the violet rays would make one oval violet image of the small circular opening in S S', as at V; the indigo rays would make an indigo image, as at I; the blue, a blue image, as at B; the green, yellow, orange, and red forming respectively a green, yellow, orange, and red image, as at G, Y, O, and R. But Newton did not find that this happened. On the contrary, the spectrum formed an unbroken rainbow-tinted streak (like a cross strip from a rainbow), fading away into darkness at the red and violet ends. He thus perceived that all violet rays are not equally refrangible, nor all indigo rays, nor are all the rays of any colour whatever equally refrangible. Hence, if a beam of rays of any colour, obtained as in the above experiment, be allowed to fall on another prism, these rays, being like the rays of sunlight, differently refrangible, may be separated. Thus, if the screen at V R (fig. 9) is perforated where the rays of any colour fall, the rays thus allowed to pass through may be received on another prism, and further dispersed; so that, instead of the image which would have fallen on the second screen but for the second prism, a lengthened image is thrown higher up. But this image shows no new colours. It is entirely red, for instance, if the hole is made in the red part of the spectrum V R. A good eye can indeed recognise a slight variation of tint in the red, which tends towards orange at the upper or most refracted part of the beam. But there is no new tint, only a slower gradation from the full red of the lower part to the slightly orange red of the upper part.

The idea occurred to Newton, however, that though the rays of any given colour are not all equally refrangible, yet the entire range of refrangibilities between the extreme red and the extreme violet may not be represented in the spectrum. There might, for instance, be a definite difference between the most refrangible red rays and the least refrangible orange rays; and in this case the extension of the process described in the last paragraph would show a gap in the spectrum between the orange and the red. And even if gaps could not be seen, yet there would not be a regular gradation of light from end to end of the spectrum. Finding after varying the experiment in different ways, and especially modifying the form of the aperture, that the spectrum still showed a uniform gradation of tints from end to end, Newton concluded that all orders of refrangibility from that of the extreme violet end to that of the extreme red end, are represented in the solar spectrum. If that were really so, the method of analysis which forms the subject of the present book could have had no existence

CHAPTER II.

DARK SPACES IN THE SPECTRUM.

WOLLASTON was the first who succeeded in showing that the solar spectrum is not continuous, as Newton had inferred from his experiments. It is probable that Newton had looked only for well-marked gaps. None such exist in the spectrum. Wollaston employed a method by which small spaces wanting in the spectrum had a fair chance of being detected; for instead of admitting light through a circular aperture (or a triangular, oblong, or other like aperture, such as Newton used in other experiments), Wollaston admitted the light through a very narrow slit parallel to the refracting edge of the prism. It will be well, while considering the effect of this change, to notice a difference in Wollaston's method of observing the spectrum. Newton's plan of receiving the spectrum on a screen, however convenient for exhibiting the spectrum, is not convenient for observing it. Wollaston observed the spectrum through the prism.

Let A (fig. 10) be a bright point of light; P a prism, through which the eye E observes the bright object A. If rays of any colour were all of the same refrangibility, the eye at E would see a red image at R by rays which had followed the course $A\,r\,r'\,E$, a violet image at V by rays which had followed the course $A\,v\,v'\,E$, and intermediate images, O (orange), Y (yellow), G (green), B (blue), and I (indigo), by rays which had followed the intermediate paths indicated in the figure. As matters actually are, instead of a series of seven images at

R, O, Y, G, B, I, V, the eye will see a blended series forming the spectrum R V, the violet appearing lowest,

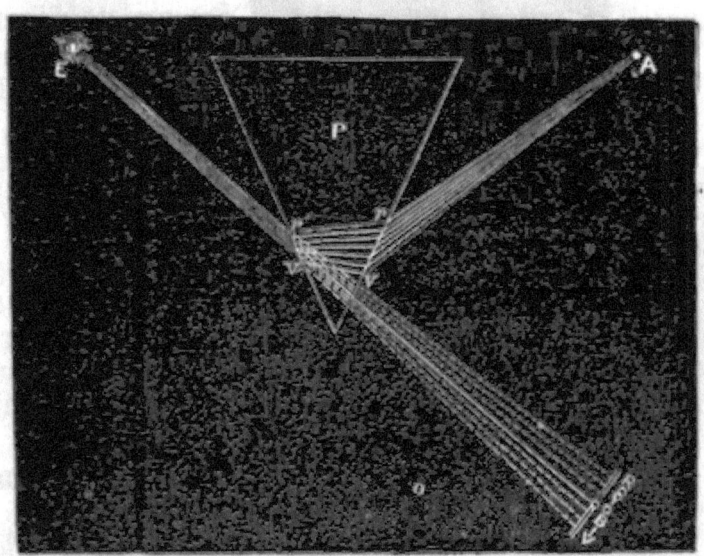

Fig. 10.—The direct examination of the prismatic spectrum.

the red appearing uppermost. In other respects this image corresponds exactly with the image thrown on a screen. Moreover, this image may be viewed, if necessary, with a telescope, instead of the naked eye.

Next let us consider the effect of the *shape* of the source of light, whether an aperture or a luminous object. Suppose there were but one image for each of the seven colours of the spectrum. Then the spectrum would be a set of seven coloured images of the source of light, arranged as shown in fig. 11. Here we see seven circles, seven triangles, seven oblongs, and seven lines of light, as the respective spectra of a circular, triangular, oblong, and linear source of light. It is clear that the space between two successive linear images is much greater than the space between two successive circular, or triangular, or oblong images. In other words, there is room for many more intermediate images. Hence if rays of certain degrees of refrangibility are really wanting, so that instead of the spectrum being formed by a perfect series of overlapping images it is really incomplete in parts, there will be a much better chance of detecting this fact if we use a fine luminous line for the source of light, or admit light through a fine slit, than where the source of light has any considerable width in the direction of the spectrum's length.

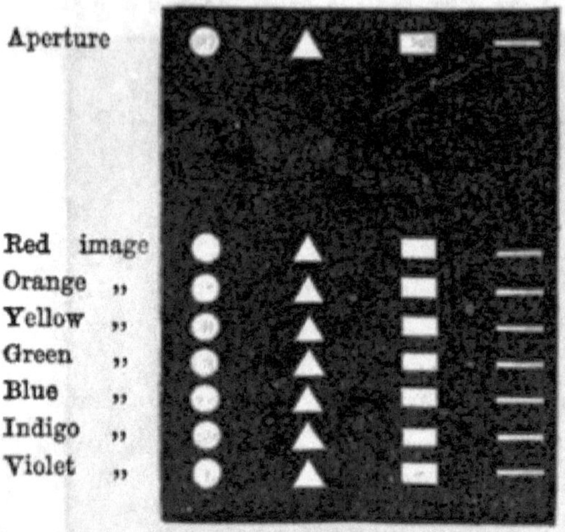

Fig. 11.—Illustrating the effect of the shape of the source of light on the character of the spectrum.

Wollaston tried the experiment. Admitting light through a narrow slit, parallel to the refracting edge of the prism, he observed the spectrum in the manner illustrated in fig. 11. He found that it was not continuous, but crossed by certain dark lines, lying at right angles to its length. In other words, light of certain definite degrees of refrangibility is absent from the solar beam.

He did not carry this inquiry further, supposing, doubtless, that the discovery was singular rather than valuable. He had no reason for suspecting that the quality he had detected indicated any property peculiar to sunlight. Still less would he suppose that when this property was traced to its source it would help to reveal the very constitution of the sun's mass.

But Fraunhofer, in 1814, examined these dark lines with such care and attention, that in recognition of his labours they have ever since been called Fraunhofer's lines. Using for source of light a much finer slit than Wollaston had employed, and studying the image, formed as in fig. 11, with a telescope instead of the unaided eye, he found many dark spaces where Wollaston had seen but few. He counted and mapped, in fact, no less than 576 dark lines.

The chief lines in the solar spectrum are indicated in fig. 12; and as reference is continually made to the lines as here lettered, the student should carefully note their position in the spectrum. A is a strong line close to the red end of the spectrum. B is a strong and rather broad line in the red. Between A and B is a band of several lines called a. C is a dark and well marked line. Between B and C, Fraunhofer counted nine fine lines; between C and D about thirty. D consists of two strong lines close together. Between D and E, Fraunhofer counted eighty-four lines. E is a band of several lines, the middle one of the set being stronger than the rest. At b are three strong lines,

Fig. 12.—The dark lines in the solar spectrum.

the two farthest from E being close together. Between E and b, Fraunhofer counted twenty-four lines, and between b and F more than fifty. The lines F, G, and H are well defined. Between F and G, Fraunhofer counted 185 lines, between G and H, 190 lines, and he found many lines between H and I, the violet end of the spectrum. I remind the reader of the importance of noting the position of the lettered lines in the spectrum, for these lines are constantly employed for reference. Let him remember, then, that A, B, and C are in the red portion of the spectrum; D is in the orange-yellow; E in the yellow-green; F in the green blue; G in the indigo; and H in the violet.

Now let us recall what these dark lines really are. They are gaps in the spectrum indicating the absence of rays of certain refrangibilities from the beam of solar light. The spectrum shown in fig. 12 is formed in reality of a series of images of the fine slit through which sunlight is received. The red part of the light, with its various degrees of refrangibility, makes a series of red images, the orange makes a series of orange images, and so on. But the red light not containing *all* the degrees of refrangibility within its limits, certain red images which should appear are wanting, leaving dark spaces, as at A, *a*, B, and C; so certain images are wanting in the orange part of the spectrum, others in the yellow, and so forth.

Fraunhofer next inquired whether the dark lines may not be due to peculiarities in the substance forming the prism. He found, however, that they may be seen with prisms of every kind of glass and crystal, as well as with prisms formed by enclosing various fluids in prism-shaped phials.

He next examined sunlight reflected in various ways; as from the moon, the planets, from clouds, the sky, terrestrial substances, and so forth. In every case he found the same lines which he had seen in the spectrum of direct sunlight. He studied the spectrum of the sun when close to the horizon, and found that the violet end of the spectrum is then very faint, and several new lines are to be found in various parts of the spectrum. He examined next the light from the fixed stars. He found that though each star gives a spectrum showing the prismatic colours, none of these spectra are exactly like the solar spectrum. Some lines in the solar spectrum are wanting in star spectra, others are less strongly marked; and some lines are seen in star spectra which are absent from the solar spectrum. No two stars seem to have exactly the same spectrum. He found that when the flame of a candle or lamp is the source of light, the spectrum shows only two dark lines, or rather one double line, in the same place as the double line D of the solar spectrum.

Before proceeding to consider the results of further

research into these dark lines in the solar and other spectra, it will be well to describe here the methods by which the spectrum is increased in length, while its purity is retained.

If light were not variously refrangible, according to its colour, but all refracted in the same degree, then when we looked at an object through a prism we should still see the object blurred, though not with the prismatic colours. For from every point of the object a diverging pencil of rays would travel, and this pencil, after being bent twice in its passage through the prism, would no longer diverge from a single point; so that instead of seeing for each point of the object a corresponding point in the image, we should have a small round spot of light, and the image made up of such spots of light would be correspondingly confused. There is only one exception to this rule, viz., when the pencil passes on such a course as D e h E in fig. 5 (p. 11) the two parts D e and h E being equally inclined to the faces of the prism at I and E. Then the emergent pencil proceeds from a single point (or very nearly so). The prism is said to be used at the angle of minimum deviation in such a case, because the deviation is less than for any other position. Now when we are examining a spectrum as in fig. 10, it is manifest that though one part may be examined at this angle of minimum deviation (the part G in the case there illustrated), and so be seen clearly, all the rest must be viewed at a different angle, and therefore less distinctly. This was not a matter of great importance in Newton's or Wollaston's experiments, where the pencils did not follow a long course through the prisms, and where the image was not very closely examined. But when greater dispersion of the rays is to be obtained by increasing the prismatic action, and where the prismatic image is to be examined telescopically, it becomes highly desirable that some method should be devised for giving a spectrum pure throughout, instead of one merely pure in one particular part. This difficulty was met by Simms, the optician, in 1830. He simply got rid of the divergence of the rays of light by placing a converging lens in such a position as to make the rays parallel. Thus let P (fig. 13) be the prism, S a point of the source of light, S L a divergent pencil of light proceeding from S. Then if a convex lens, L L′, be so placed that the pencil after passing through the lens consists of parallel rays, these parallel rays, falling at $i\,i'$, on the surface $i\,i''$ of the prism, are equally refracted, and therefore continue parallel as they pass to $e\,e'$, where they are equally refracted at emergence, and thus the emergent beam $e\,e'$ R consists of parallel rays. This beam will still continue parallel after being refracted through a second prism, or through any number of prisms, and the image of S will be truly seen by beams which have gone through one or more prisms. This being appreciably true for all rays of all colours, the whole series of images of S forming the spectrum will be truly formed; or, in other words, all parts of the spectrum will be seen with equal distinctness.* The lens L L′ used for this purpose is called the *collimating* lens. Fig. 14 shows how a telescope is used in combination

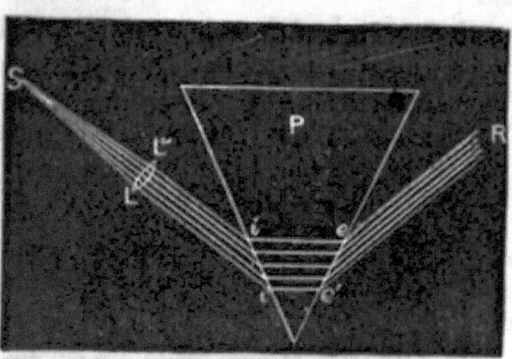

Fig. 13.—Illustrating Simms's device for purifying the solar spectrum.

* Persons unacquainted with the laws of optics sometimes suppose that Newton's discovery of the advantage of using the angle of minimum deviation is important for modern work with the spectroscope. Thus I have seen it stated in an elementary treatise on the spectroscope that "our spectroscope depends" *inter alia* on this discovery. But in reality the invention of the collimating lens removes entirely the difficulty which Newton partially met by using the prism at the angle of minimum deviation, and enables the observer to use the prism at other angles with equal effect.

with a collimating lens. The light emitted from the source of light, after passing through the slit seen at the extremity of the left hand tube, is converged into parallelism by the lens of this tube, and after passing through the prism, falls on the object glass of the telescope on the right, and is acted upon precisely as the rays from a distant object are acted on by the object-glass and eye-piece of a telescope. Comparing fig. 13 with figs. 10 and 14, it will be noticed that the use of a collimating lens and observing telescope are simply

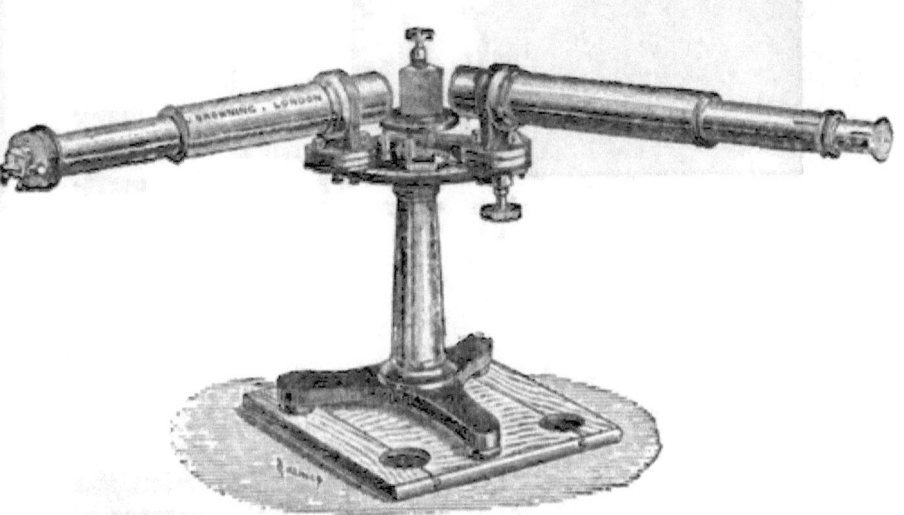

Fig. 14.—A spectroscope of one prism with collimating tube and observing telescope.

devices for first purifying the spectrum R V of fig. 10, and then observing it with suitable telescopic power.

When the rays have been made parallel by means of a collimating lens, any number of prisms may be used to increase the dispersion of the rays. The effect of several prisms in increasing the dispersion is illustrated in fig. 15, where light received through the slit S S' is supposed to be carried round a battery of four prisms, with increase of dispersion at each, until finally it forms a spectrum on the screen *a b*. In the figure only seven spectral images of the slit are shown— V, the violet image, by rays which have been most refracted; R, the red image, by rays which have been least refracted, and the rest in intermediate positions. It will be seen that such a way of using many prisms would in some sense correspond with the effect of removing the screen further away from the source of light in Newton's original experiment. Although no screen is used by spectroscopists, but the emergent rays received into a telescope, as shown in fig. 14, it will be convenient in what follows to refer to a spectrum supposed to be received on a screen, as in fig. 15.

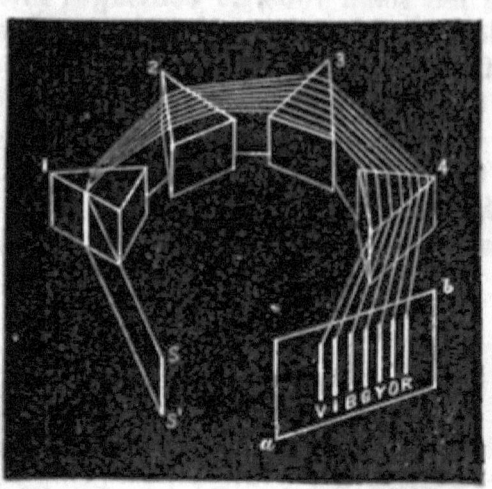

Fig. 15.—Showing how several prisms may be used to increase the dispersion.

It is easy to see why with increase of dispersion the dark lines are more clearly shown. If the increase of dispersion merely made the spectrum longer, without modifying its nature, very little would be gained. But it is easy to see that more than this is done. Let it be remembered that in the spectrum we have a series of images of the slit, and that our chance of detecting the absence of certain rays from the solar beam depends on the recognition of a space in the spectrum where no image is formed. Now let *a b c* (fig. 16, I.) represent a small part of the spectrum as it would be if the slit, instead of having definite though small breadth, were an actual line. Then the light corresponding to the two edges of the dark space *b* forms in the real spectrum two images of the slit, as at B, where these images are of such a width as to touch, leaving no dark space between them. But now suppose we increase the dispersive power, and get a spectrum of greater length, as at II. Then the parts *a b c* of the true spectrum, that is, an absolutely pure spectrum, are correspondingly increased in length; while in the spectrum as actually seen the two images of the slit formed by light corresponding to the edges of the dark space *b* are formed as at B and B', no broader than they were before, for their breadth is that of the slit, but thrown farther apart, so that a dark space now appears between them.

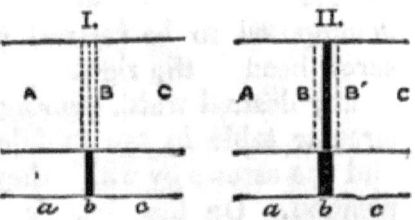

Fig. 16.—Illustrating the effects of increased dispersion.

We see, then, how important it is to increase the dispersive power of a battery of prisms for examining sunlight, or any light in the spectrum of which are large numbers of dark lines. For thus, as illustrated in fig. 16 at I. and II., dark lines may be seen, which otherwise would escape detection. And again, two dark lines very close together, which would appear as one with low dispersive power, may be shown clearly separated with a higher power. And, as we shall presently see, a still more important advantage of increased dispersion in certain branches of spectroscopic research resides in the power thus afforded of determining the true position of particular lines in the spectrum.

To secure a spectrum as pure as possible, and showing many dark lines, we require first to have the slit through which light is admitted as fine as possible, next a collimating lens to make the rays parallel, then a battery of several prisms, and lastly, a telescope for examining the spectrum.

A battery of two prisms constructed to meet these

requirements is shown in fig. 17. On the left we see the collimating tube, its left extremity carrying the contrivance for forming a slit of any desired width. The slit is supposed to be vertical in the figure, and the little screw head to the right of it is turned to adjust the slit to any desired width (see fig. 40, p. 56). On the little circular table in the middle the two prisms are seen, and the screws by which they are secured in any desired position. On the right is the telescope for observing

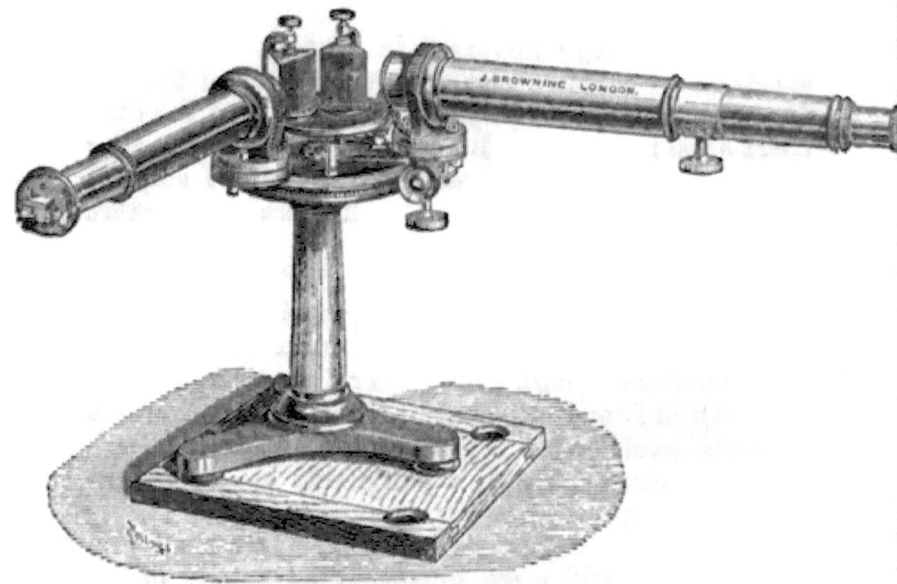

Fig. 17.—A spectroscope with two prisms.

the spectrum. This telescope can be swept round (remaining horizontal), being carried on a bar seen underneath the prisms, and thus different parts of the spectrum can be examined. Of the two screw heads seen underneath the telescope near its larger end, one works this slow movement, the other serves to clamp the telescope. The third screw towards the eye-end is for focal adjustment, to make the spectrum as clear as possible to the observer's eye.

The instrument used by Kirchhoff, to whom science owes the great discovery which has made spectroscopic analysis what it is, contained four prisms.

It is evident that where several prisms are used to secure considerable dispersion, a part only of the spectrum can be advantageously studied. A certain portion of the rays emerging from the last prism of the battery fall centrally on the object-glass of the telescope. The rest fall obliquely, and give a less distinct,

Fig. 18.—Browning's automatic spectroscope.

as well as a less luminous, image of the part of the spectrum to which they belong. Hence it is desirable to have an arrangement by which each part of the spectrum can be viewed equally well by rays which, after passing round the battery symmetrically, fall centrally on the object glass of the observing telescope. To effect this, not only the observing telescope itself, but the prisms, require to be movable; for though we no longer require to have the prisms arranged for minimum deviation to secure distinctness of the image, it is clear that when they are so arranged we get the maximum amount of light through the prisms.

To meet this difficulty various plans have been devised for communicating suitable motions to the prisms,

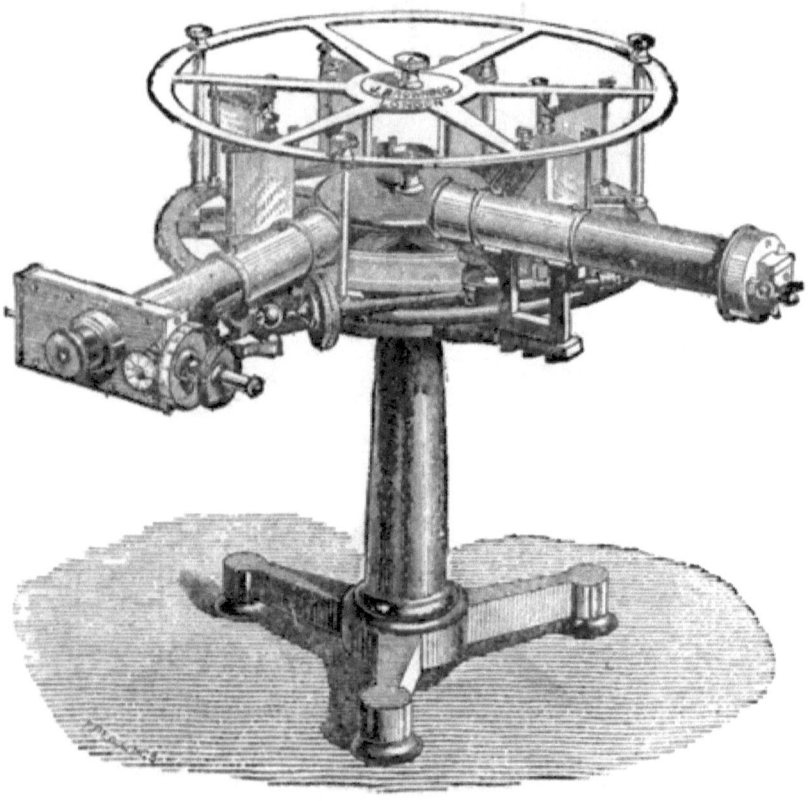

Fig. 19.

the best (in fact the only plan which, with a slight modification presently to be described, exactly fulfils the required condition of minimum deviation) being the one illustrated in fig. 18, due to the inventive genius of Mr. Browning, F.R.A.S., the eminent optician. Of the six prisms, the first is attached to the ground plate; the others are connected at their corners in the way shown in the figure, the observing telescope (the left hand tube) being attached to one corner of the sixth prism. To each prism is attached a slotted bar, square to its base, and a movable central pin passes through all the slots. It is easily seen that, as the telescope is carried round (guided by a slot), the prisms move in such a way as always to have their bases equidistant from the central pin, and so to form a symmetrical battery.

Fig. 19 shows this instrument as at present made by Mr. Browning. The reader will have no difficulty in distinguishing its various parts.

In the original arrangement of this automatic or self-adjusting spectroscope the first prism was fixed, and, although the battery itself is always symmetrical, yet, as the first prism remained in an unchanged position, it is evident there could not be minimum deviation, and therefore maximum illumination, for all parts of the spectrum. The consideration of this circumstance in the original plan led me to suggest a slight alteration in the addition of a straight slot in the plate at right angles to the path of the rays incident on the first prism. If, then, only one corner of this prism is attached to the plate, but the prism is movable around that corner, as shown in fig. 20, this prism moves with the rest, and it can be proved that as a result all the prisms assume the position for minimum deviation, whatever part of the spectrum is under examination.

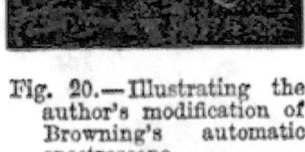

Fig. 20.—Illustrating the author's modification of Browning's automatic spectroscope.

The action of an automatic spectroscope constructed according to this plan is illustrated in fig. 21, where E E' is the emergent beam.

Although this automatic movement places a battery of prisms in the most favourable condition for showing the spectrum with maximum dispersion, yet it is clear that there is a limit to the dispersion which can be obtained with a single battery. Thus when the light has been bent round a nearly complete circle of prisms, as in fig. 21, the emergent light E E' will be intercepted by the first prism of the battery, and this circumstance limits the dispersion which can be given in this manner.

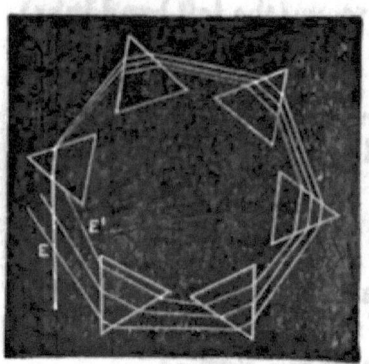

Fig. 21.—Illustrating the limited power of a single circular battery of prisms.

The dispersive power of a battery of prisms may be doubled by carrying the rays twice through the battery. This may be done by making the last prism of the battery right-angled and half the size of the others, as shown in fig. 22, and causing the rays which fall on the face D C to be there reflected, passing again through the battery, and falling eventually upon the collimating lens. Another reflection is required to send the light out at right angles to the axis of the collimating tube to an eye-piece suitably placed for observing it.

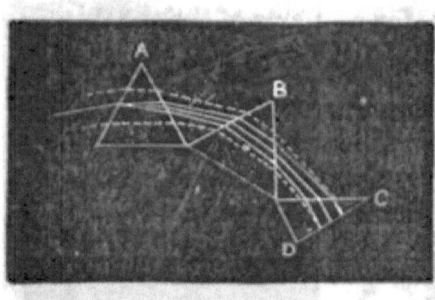

Fig. 22.—Illustrating methods for carrying the rays twice through a battery of prisms.

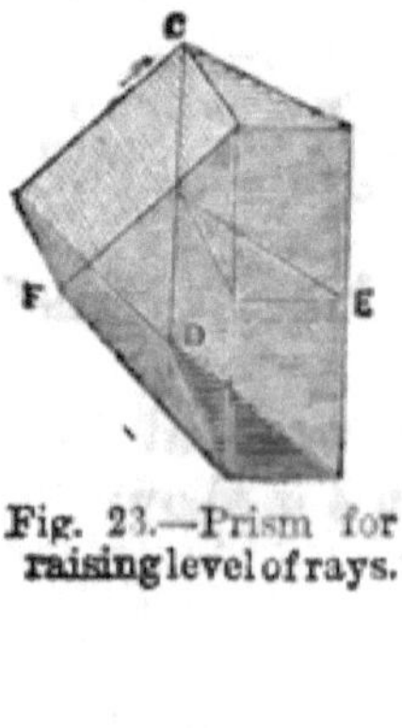

A better plan, though more costly, is to have all the prisms of the battery of twice the usual height, and for the last using a half prism, as C D E of fig. 23, to which a right-angled prism C F D is added. The rays which pass through the face E D are totally reflected upwards by the face F D, and again totally reflected horizon-

Fig. 23.—Prism for raising level of rays.

tally by the face C F, so passing out through the face E C (which forms with E D a single face C E D). Apart from the action of the compound prism C E F in carrying the rays to a higher level, the dispersion produced as the rays pass through the two halves of the face C E D is equal to the dispersion produced by the single prism of which E C D is the half.

But in examining sunlight, almost any amount of dispersion may be used, and still leave more than enough light. It is desirable, therefore, to have even a

Fig. 24.—The author's double-double battery of prisms.

stronger battery than one in which the rays are bent round a complete circle and back again. Accordingly I devised the plan illustrated in fig. 24. Here the automatic method is extended to a second battery, while either method for returning the rays illustrated in figs. 22 and 23 is employed to double the dispersive power of the double battery thus obtained. A B is the light incident on the first prism of the first battery, and the course of the light can be traced by the triple set of lines through the double set of prisms, the dotted return lines showing the course of the return rays, which emerge at C C'. The large intermediate prism D E belongs to both batteries. There is no loss of light in passing from one battery to the other, because the reflection at D D' is total. This double-double battery has a dispersive power equal to that of nineteen equilateral prisms.*

There are methods also by which dispersion can be secured without that continual bending of the rays in one direction which tends to bring the course of the rays (as in fig. 25) athwart their original direction.

Fig. 25.—Herschel's direct-vision spectroscope.

Thus, if we use a right-angled prism, such as *a b c* in fig. 25, letting the beam of light pass through on such a course as is there shown by the broken line E F, we get dispersion without deviation. There is refraction and consequent dispersion as the light enters at the face *a b*, total reflection at the faces *b c* and *a c*, and refraction, with additional dispersion, as the ray emerges from the face *b c*, the two reflections having just cor-

* It is rather a singular circumstance, perhaps, in the history of this S-shaped battery, that when I designed it I had never even seen a spectroscope, showing that it is not absolutely necessary to have handled and used a scientific instrument to be able to devise a practicable extension of its powers. Mr. Browning made a battery on this design, and Mr. W. Spottiswoode, who purchased the instrument, lent it to Mr. Huggins. It so chanced, by another somewhat singular coincidence, that I saw the solar spectrum (at least a well-dispersed spectrum) for the first time with this very instrument.

rected the deviations produced by the two refractions. Again, we may combine two such prisms, as *a b c* in fig. 25, in such a way (see fig. 26) that the emergent ray is not merely parallel to the incident ray, but actually coincident with that ray in direction. Unfortunately there is a difficulty in practice arising from the largeness of the number of refractions and reflections, and the difficulty of making the angles *a* and *c* exactly correct.

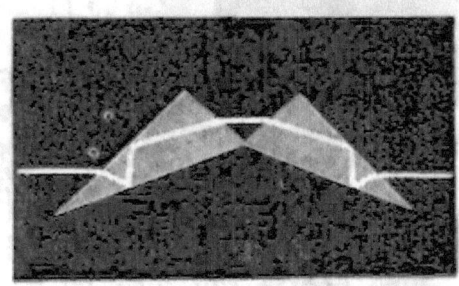

Fig. 26.—The Herschel-Browning combination of prisms.

A more convenient plan in practice was devised by Amici. It depends on the fact that the refractive powers of different media are not proportional to their dispersive power. If the deviation produced by a prism always bore a constant proportion to the dispersion of the rays, whatever the substance of the prism, then we could not by any combination of prisms see the spectrum of any luminous object when looking directly at that object. For the very fact that there was no deviation of the rays from the object would imply that there was no dispersion. But as this proportion has been found not to hold, we can get dispersion without deviation. Thus a prism of flint glass gives a spectrum of much greater length for a given deviation of the mean rays than a prism of crown glass. If, then, we were to correct the deviation caused by a flint glass prism by means of a crown glass prism, so placed as to cause an equal deviation in the opposite direction, we should still have a balance of uncorrected dispersion; in other words, a spectrum would be visible. Amici's compound prism, shown in fig. 27, effects this with the least possible loss of light. Here a flint glass prism P' is placed between two crown glass prisms, P and *p*, to which it is cemented with Canada balsam, a transparent cement. The rays of mean refrangibility suffer no deviation, so that it is possible to look directly at a luminous object through the compound prism. The two prisms P and *p* cause a dispersion in one direction, while the prism P′ causes a greater dispersion in the opposite direction, and thus a spectrum is seen, such as would be produced by a prism placed like P′, but of much smaller refracting angle.

Fig. 27.—Amici's direct-vision compound prism.

Five prisms can also be combined into a single direct-vision series, as shown in fig. 28. Here the first, third, and fifth prisms are of crown glass. The two others, P′ and P, of flint glass. This arrangement was first used by Janssen.

Fig. 28.—Janssen's extension of Amici's direct-vision method.

Browning combines seven prisms in a similar way, making a spectroscope of singularly excellent performance considering its small dimensions. The complete instrument is pictured in fig. 29, the compound prism

Fig. 29.—Browning's miniature spectroscope.

being within the sliding tube whose end is seen towards the left. The slit is seen on the right. It can be widened or narrowed, by turning round the ring with milled edge seen at the same end of the spectroscope.

The entire instrument is only about 3½ inches in length, so that it can be put into the waistcoat pocket.

Compound direct vision prisms can be combined with a single prism forming a battery. Sometimes also compound prisms are used, which, though not giving direct vision, give considerable dispersion for small deviation, so that a very powerful battery of them may be formed without bringing the emergent rays athwart the rays which fall on the first prism. A compound prism of this sort is shown in fig. 30. P is a prism of flint glass, and $p\,p'$ are two prisms of crown glass. These two prisms without much reducing the dispersion caused by P, considerably reduce the deviation.

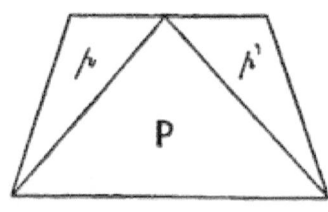

Fig. 30.—Compound prism for securing considerable dispersion with small deviation.

Fig. 31 presents a combination devised by Dr. Rutherfurd of New York, for whom Mr. Browning constructed a compound prism of this kind.

I have arranged a combination of compound prisms on the same plan as my automatic twice-acting double battery (fig. 24).

Fig. 31.—Dr. Rutherfurd's compound prism.

A spectroscope constructed on this plan would be more powerful than any yet made.

The method of reversing the direction of a beam, carrying it to a higher level by means of such a prism as is shown in fig. 23, may obviously be repeated, carrying the beam backwards and forwards through the same battery, until sufficient dispersion has been obtained. But though the automatic action would thus be simplified, the tall prisms required could not be very easily constructed.

A prism used as in the case illustrated in fig. 7, the incident light falling perpendicular to the first face magnifies an object seen through it with light of one colour, the magnifying taking place in one direction only however, namely, in that corresponding to the length of the spectrum. A half prism so used that the incident light falls perpendicular to the shorter face acts in this way. Turned the other way a half prism diminishes (in the same direction) an object seen with monochromatic light. The distance between two neighbouring lines would be increased in the former case and diminished in the latter, an effect which must be carefully distinguished from increase or diminution of dispersion. The same holds for compound prisms. Mr. W. H. M. Christie, assistant-observer at Greenwich, has had some spectroscopes made of half prisms, simple or compound. Professor Eaton, and other American spectroscopists, had preceded him in this respect. In cases where it is important to increase the separation between lines as in the method dealt with at pp. 114 and 115, and in other cases where it may be convenient to have the spectrum shortened without impairing its purity, the use of half prisms is advantageous. But they cannot be effectively substituted for full prisms, used at the angle of minimum deviation, where great dispersion is required.

One other point had better be considered in this place, before we pass on to the researches which resulted in explaining the meaning of the lines in the solar spectrum.

It is often necessary to have some means of determining the position of lines observed in the spectrum. Several methods may be employed for this purpose. The simplest, and most usual, is to have, besides the collimating tube and the observing telescope, a third tube, somewhat like the collimating tube, so placed that the rays from a light after passing through a transparent plate, on which a fine scale is engraved, and through a lens, by which they are made parallel, are reflected at the nearest face of the last prism of the battery, and pass into the telescope along with the beam of light under analysis. Thus the eye while viewing the spectrum of this light through the telescope sees also a magnified image of the fine scale. The third tube can be adjusted by means of a screw, so that any line in the scale may be brought into agreement with a known line in the spectrum, and then the exact distance of some other line from the former can be determined in parts of the scale. Or, if convenient, the distance between any two lines in the spectrum can be at once observed without shifting the scale.

For the illuminated scale a micrometer is sometimes substituted. By turning a screw-head a slit or fine wire may be brought into coincidence with any line of the spectrum. The amount of motion necessary to carry the slit or wire from one line to another of the spectrum is indicated by the marks on the screw-head.

Since the fine scale in one case, or the micrometer mark in the other, is seen by means of the observing telescope, it is necessary for distinctness of vision that the rays which are reflected at the last face of the prism should be parallel, like those which emerge from that face to form the image of the spectrum. Hence it is necessary to have a lens at the end of the small tube, just as there is a lens at the end of the collimating tube. Each lens serves the same purpose, namely, to make those rays parallel which before reaching the lens were divergent.

The relative position of the lines of a spectrum may also be determined by providing the observing telescope with a cross wire or line of light, which can be brought into coincidence with any line of the spectrum by shifting the telescope. The amount of motion necessary for this purpose indicates the distance of the line from the part of the spectrum to which the telescope had been directed before the motion began.

The reader can now understand the purpose of the various portions of a compound spectroscope such as is shown in fig. 32, which represents the spectroscope made by Mr. J. Browning for the Kew Observatory.

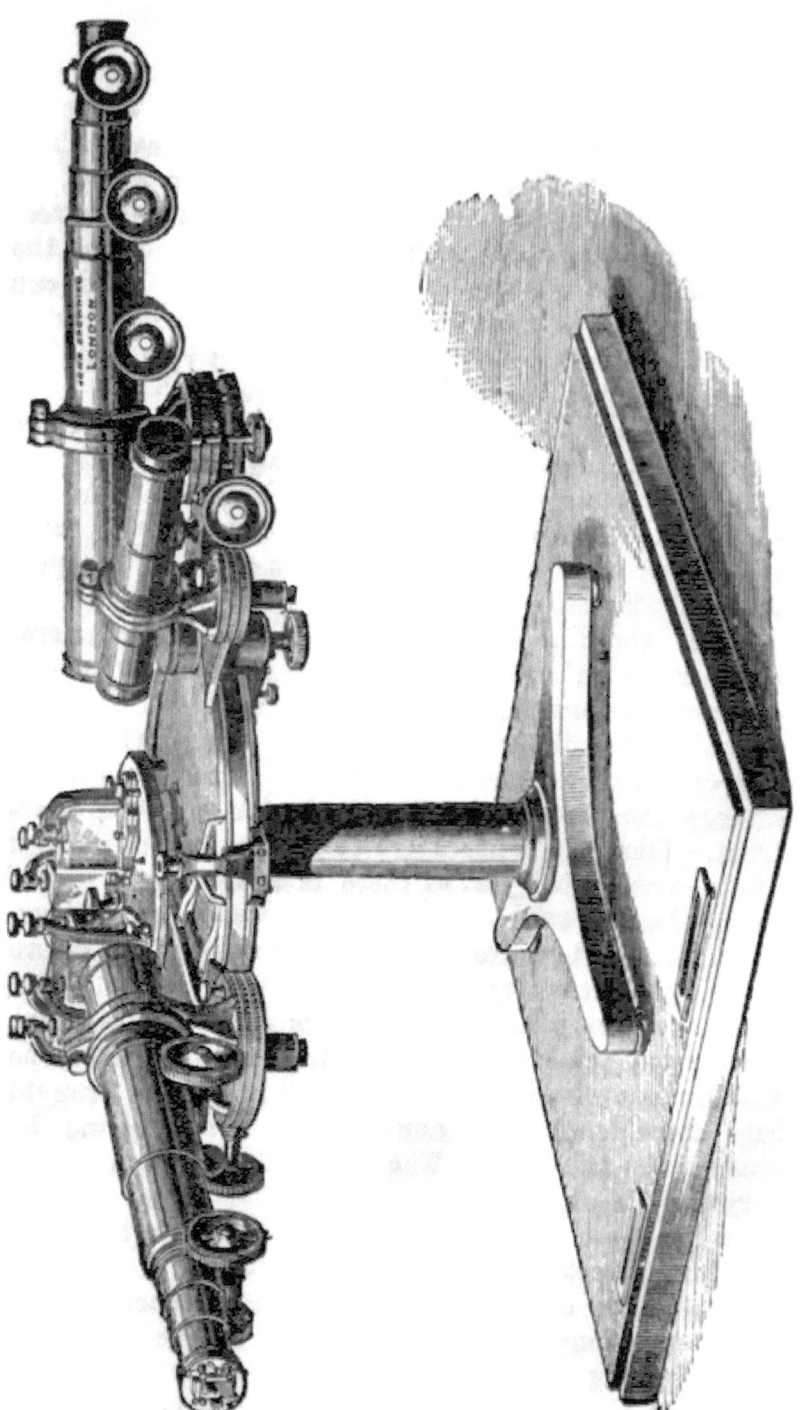

Fig. 32.—The Kew spectroscope (made by Browning).

On the left is the collimating tube. The tube bearing the maker's name is the observing telescope. The third tube, the shortest of the three, carries the scale to be illuminated by a lamp so placed as to cast its light down the tube. On the table to which the three tubes are attached is seen the battery of prisms, arranged so that the rays pass through them in the way shown in fig. 21.

CHAPTER III.

VARIOUS ORDERS OF SPECTRA.

We have learned from Fraunhofer's observations that various sources of light give different spectra. We must now consider this point more particularly. Not only does the history of spectroscopic analysis bring the point specially before us at this stage, but the treatment of the subject as a science, and without reference to what may be regarded as accidents in the progress of discovery, requires that we should now examine the various orders of spectra obtained from different luminous bodies.

In the first place, it is to be noticed that solid and fluid bodies glowing with intensity of heat give a spectrum without dark lines or gaps of any sort, or what is called a continuous spectrum. The spectrum, however, is not the same for all degrees of heat. Thus, if a piece of metal is gradually heated, it will be found that as soon as the metal glows with a dull red heat the red part of the spectrum begins to be seen; as the heat increases, the orange part of the spectrum appears (the red part not disappearing, but, on the contrary, showing more brightly); and with gradually increasing heat, the yellow, green, blue, indigo, and violet portions of the spectrum successively appear, until at last the whole length of the spectrum is seen from the extreme red to the extreme violet. At this time the metal viewed with the naked eye appears brilliantly white.

Whatever solid or liquid substance is the source of light, the spectrum is always continuous, though the brilliancy of different parts of the spectrum is not always the same, or similarly proportioned. Two exceptions have been noted—in the case of the substances Erbia and Didymium—where certain bright bands are seen in the spectrum, which, without destroying its continuity, give to it a character resembling that of another order of spectra presently to be described; but it appears that these are not real exceptions, the bright bands not being really due to glowing solid substances. We may take this then for a general rule that the light from glowing solid and liquid bodies gives a continuous spectrum.*

Seeing that the nature of the continuous spectrum given by a glowing solid or liquid body depends on the heat of the body, and that the spectrum only begins to be seen at the red end when the heat has reached a certain amount, the question is suggested, Are the limits of the spectrum we see the real limits of the range over which the effects emitted by the luminous body are dispersed by prismatic refraction? We *see* the light, and our eyesight thus informs us that certain effects are produced in those particular directions which lie between the red and violet ends of the spectrum; but might not some more delicate or some different method of observation indicate effects produced beyond the red and beyond the violet extremities of the visible spectrum? The commotion of the particles of a body by which it becomes luminous *does* cause other effects also. Thus, almost every self-luminous body gives out

---

* Schellen somewhat illogically gives the converse of this rule, after stating the facts which establish the rule itself. "It may *therefore* be considered," he says, "that, as a rule, where there is a continuous spectrum without gaps, and containing every shade of colour, the light is derived from an incandescent solid or liquid body." This mistake is not important in itself, for the rule chances to be nearly just. But reasoning of this sort is carefully to be avoided by the learner. To prove that solid and liquid bodies give continuous spectra is not equivalent to proving that bodies which give continuous spectra are necessarily solid or liquid.

heat* along with its light; and again, nearly all self-luminous bodies produce chemical changes in substances of suitable sensitiveness on which their rays fall. Spectroscopic analysis, besides sifting the rays of one colour from those of another, is able to sift out rays which do not produce the sensation called light from those which do; and it is thus found that beyond the red end of the spectrum rays fall which produce heat, while beyond the violet end rays fall which produce certain chemical effects. Let the reader be careful not to attach a definiteness to this statement which it does not really possess. It does not assert that the luminous rays produce no heat, or that chemical action is peculiar to rays beyond the violet end. All that it asserts is, that rays beyond the red end are found to have a heating effect, and that rays beyond the violet end are found to produce certain chemical effects.

The actual relation between the heat and light of various parts of the spectrum is shown in fig. 33. The curve marked L indicates the intensity of light in different parts of the spectrum. A little to the left of A is the red end of the spectrum, and we see the light curve springing here from the horizontal upper edge of the spectrum. Between the Fraunhofer lines D and E the spectrum is brightest, and we see the light curve carried here to its farthest range from that horizontal line; it gradually draws nearer towards the right, and reaches the horizontal line a little to the right of H, showing that there lies the violet end of the visible spectrum. The curved line marked H indicates in the same way the heating effect of various portions of the spectrum, and it will be observed that this effect is greatest beyond the visible red end of the spectrum, but that the heat curve extends nearly to the visible violet end of the spectrum. It should be noticed, however, that in estimating the heat received from

---

* Possibly every self-luminous body gives out some degree of heat; but in some cases, as of phosphorescence, &c., the presence of heat is not readily determined.

various parts of the spectrum, the dispersive action of the prism, and also the quality of the substance of the prism in transmitting heat, ought to be considered. For instance, rays of a certain colour which possess in reality before they fall on the prism a certain heating power, may be partially deprived of that power by the absorptive action of the glass of which the prism is made, and may also, by being exceptionally dispersed, appear to have a relatively smaller heating power than they actually possess. The heat curve H of fig. 33

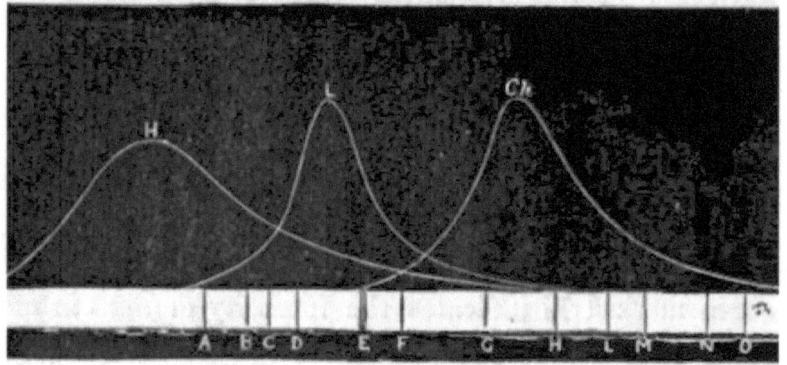

Fig. 33.—Illustrating the heating, luminous, and chemical activity of various parts of the solar spectrum.

would be considerably modified if these considerations were fairly taken into account.

The curve Ch is commonly described as representing the chemical energy of the rays belonging to various parts of the spectrum. It has in reality, however, been determined solely with reference to that particular kind of chemical energy called actinism, which produces those changes in certain sensitive substances on which the photographic art depends. It will be observed that this kind of energy attains its maximum just within the visible violet end of the spectrum. But similar remarks apply to the curve Ch as to the curve H, and, indeed, to L. The determination of the heating, luminous, and chemical power of rays of different refrangibility has hitherto been but roughly effected.

Having learned that solid and liquid bodies give, when luminous, a continuous spectrum, let us inquire next what spectrum is given by vaporous bodies when glowing. The inquiry has a special bearing on the subject of the analysis of light, because light is resolved by spectrum analysis into its component colours, and it is a characteristic peculiarity of glowing vapours that they usually show well-marked colours. When we see that coloured light comes from a glowing substance, we infer that the light, when analysed with the spectroscope, will either show an *excess* of rays from the corresponding part of the spectrum, or else will be found to consist entirely of rays from certain definite parts of the spectrum. The answer given by the spectroscope to our inquiry is very significant. It is found that light from glowing vapours, instead of forming a continuous spectrum, gives a spectrum of coloured lines (images of the slit) or bands, with dark spaces intervening.

It will be well to consider here the various ways in which the spectrum of a glowing vapour may be obtained. The point chiefly to be attended to is the degree of heat necessary to vapourise the substance, and to cause its vapour to glow with light. Some substances can be examined very readily, because no great heat is required. Thus, the spectrum of sodium can be examined with a common spirit-lamp. If we put a little ordinary table-salt, which is a chloride of this metal, on a small metal spatula, and hold the salt in the flame of a spirit-lamp, the flame will immediately begin to burn with an orange-yellow light. If we examine this light with a small spectroscope (one of Browning's miniature spectroscopes, for example), then, instead of the rainbow-tinted spectrum observed when the instrument is directed to the sky or any object in sunlight, we see a strong line in the orange-yellow part of the spectrum (see the third spectrum in the coloured frontispiece). But indeed, this bright line of sodium can be seen with still simpler means, for if a piece of paper or wood be burned, the light examined with a small spectroscope shows intermittently the yellow line of sodium, that element being present in nearly all organic substances.

Usually, however, a Bunsen's gas burner lamp is required. In a lamp of this construction a pipe conveys ordinary coal-gas to the burner. A lower chamber is perforated to admit the outer air, which rises with the gas to the top of the tube. The result of this admixture is, that the gas when lighted burns with intense heat. The flame gives out little light, because of the complete combustion of carbon particles, which with less heat, as in the ordinary gas flame, would glow with light, and being solid bodies, would give a continuous spectrum, masking the spectrum of any element we wished to examine.

A still greater heat can be obtained, if necessary, by the use of a powerful blow-pipe, the air being forced through a tube communicating with a bellows, or with a vessel containing compressed air. The flame can be regulated, but when at its greatest intensity is capable of melting most of the metals. If hydrogen is used instead of coal-gas, the blow-pipe will melt even platinum; or if coal-gas is used, but oxygen instead of air, platinum can be melted. When hydrogen and oxygen are used, we get the oxyhydrogen flame, which is of still greater intensity. In this flame, platinum wire melts like wax.

But for many purposes, and in particular when it is required to exhibit spectra to an audience, resort must be had to electricity. When the electric spark flashes between two poles, one charged with positive, the other with negative electricity, it indicates that the particles lying on the course pursued by the spark are raised to an intense heat. When the electrical tension which causes the discharge is sufficiently great, the particles of the metallic poles are vapourised, and the electric spark is tinged with colour due to the metallic vapour. Thus the spectra of various metals (by which is always to be understood the spectra of their *vapours*) can be readily examined. Again, the gas or gases through which the discharge takes place are made luminous, and if enclosed in glass tubes, the light thus obtained is sufficient to show the spectrum of the gas. The spectra of the vapours of various liquids can also be obtained by placing one of the metallic poles in the liquid, and the other near enough to the surface of the liquid for the spark to pass from the surface to this pole, volatilising a small portion of the liquid. In all these cases we have a spark, whose light is *partly* that of the glowing vapour of the substance under examination, so that the spectrum of the spark includes the spectrum of this substance. Moreover, it is not difficult to determine what part is due to this substance, and what to others. For by varying the conditions we can get the spectrum of the substance in combination with various other spectra, and whatever portion of the various compound spectra thus obtained is common to all, may be inferred to be the spectrum of the one substance present in all the sparks—that is, of the substance under examination.

An electric lamp for exhibiting the spectra of metals to large audiences is shown in fig. 34. On the left is the lamp, a portion of one side being removed to show the various component parts—the upright, bearing carbon points between which the electric spark passes, metallic reflector, nozzle,

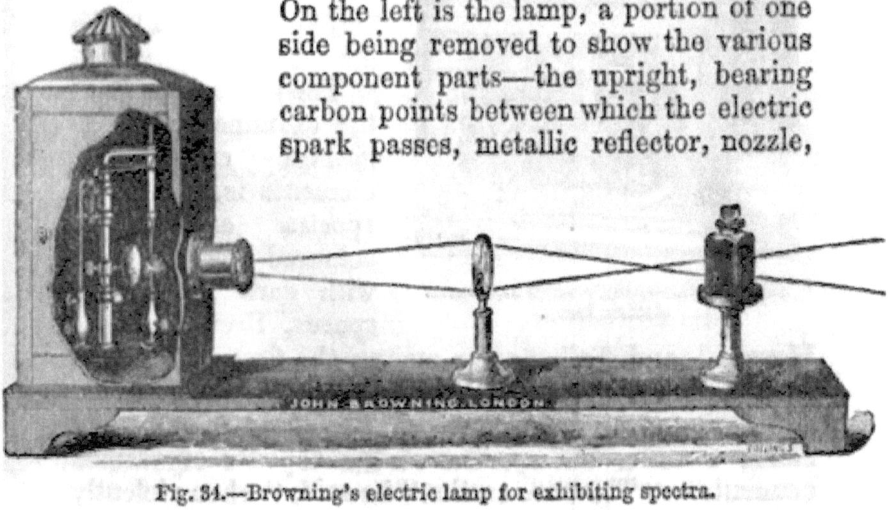

Fig. 34.—Browning's electric lamp for exhibiting spectra.

&c. In the middle is a focussing lens mounted on a stand, and on the right is a small prism-shaped phial containing bisulphide of carbon, a liquid which possesses great dispersive power, and so forms a long horizontal spectrum, with as little loss of light by absorption as possible.

A larger electric lamp is shown in fig. 35, indicating more clearly how the electric spark appears between the carbon points. Here also the wires are seen (below on the left) which convey the electric current from the battery of cells. A small quantity of the substance whose spectrum is required is placed on the lower carbon point, and when the distance between the points is suitably adjusted the light of the electric spark comes chiefly from the glowing vapour of the substance.

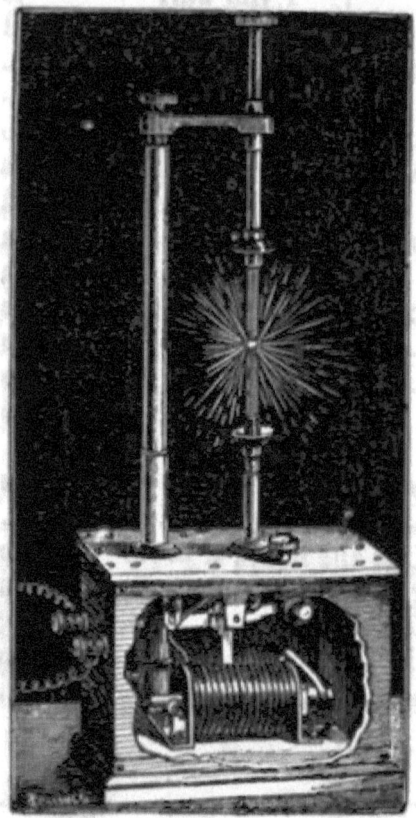

Fig. 35.—Browning's large automatic electric lamp.

The general result of the examination of the spectra of various elements is, that these spectra consist of coloured lines or bands, with dark intervening spaces. Brewster, John Herschel, and Talbot were among the first to examine such spectra. In 1822, Sir John Herschel called attention to the importance of the study of lines and bands forming the spectra of the vapours of various elements. "The pure earths," he said, "when violently heated, yield from their surfaces lights of extraordinary splendour, which, when examined by prismatic analysis, are found to possess the peculiar definite rays in excess which characterise the tints of the flames coloured by them; so that there can be no doubt that these tints arise from the molecules of the colouring matter reduced to vapour, and held in a state of violent ignition."

The coloured frontispiece gives the spectra of several elements. The first spectrum in this plate is that of the sun, showing, however, only the principal dark lines. The second is the spectrum of potassium (K or Ka, from kalium), consisting of a strong red line, another faint red line, and a strong violet line. The third is the spectrum of sodium (na. for natrium), consisting of a strong double yellow-orange line (only the most characteristic lines of the spectra are shown; with a high temperature the spectrum of sodium is found to contain several faint lines, besides the characteristic double yellow line, shown single in the plate). The fourth spectrum is that of lithium, consisting of a brilliant red line, and a fainter line of orange yellow. The fifth spectrum is that of calcium, consisting of a very bright orange line, a faint red line, several lines of yellow and yellow green, and one indigo line. The sixth spectrum, which is that of strontium, serves to indicate the effectiveness of spectrum analysis as a means of distinguishing substances whose vapours shine with the same colour; for while no one can mistake this spectrum for that of lithium, next but one above in the plate, the strontium flame can only be distinguished from the lithium flame by an eye very skilful to detect slight differences of tint, both flames being of a brilliant crimson colour. The next spectrum shown in the plate is that of barium. Then come thallium and indium, which elements are interesting as having been first detected by means of their characteristic lines, whence their names (thallium, from the Greek for a green twig, and indium for indigo) were derived. The next two spectra belong to other orders, but the last three illustrate the spectra of vapours. No. 12 is the spectrum of hydrogen at low pressure; No. 13 is a spectrum of nitrogen; and lastly, No. 14 is the spectrum of coal gas.

We have seen that the spectrum given by a solid or liquid body, though always continuous, varies according to the condition of the body with respect to temperature. Similarly the discontinuous spectrum given by a glowing vapour varies with the heat of the vapour. Thus taking the spectrum of potassium (No. 2 in the frontispiece), the brilliant red line is well seen when the ordinary Bunsen burner is used; it disappears when the temperature is raised by the blow-pipe; but it is seen again when the intense heat of the electric spark is employed. When sodium is examined at moderate temperatures, the double yellow line only is seen, but at very high temperatures so many lines are seen that the spectrum appears continuous. Plücker and Hittorf obtained similar results with the spectra of luminous gases. Thus hydrogen at very low pressure is found to give a spectrum of several fine green lines (in six groups). At higher pressure the spectrum of three lines shown in the frontispiece (No. 12) is seen. With further increase of pressure changes take place which lead to the appearance of bands. When the pressure is sufficiently increased, a continuous spectrum is seen extending from the orange to the violet, and brightest where the green line of hydrogen is situated. At higher pressure still a brilliant continuous spectrum appears. Nitrogen shows similar changes. At a certain density the spectrum of numerous bands changes to that shown in No. 13 of the coloured plate. Nitrogen also at a sufficiently high temperature and pressure gives a continuous spectrum.

But while variations such as these exist between the spectra given by the same glowing vapour at different temperatures and pressures, and while a vapour at a very high temperature and pressure may give a spectrum appreciably continuous, the general law remains that the spectra of glowing vapours consist of bright lines or bands occupying definite positions. Here then we have a means of distinguishing a glowing solid or liquid body from a glowing gas or vapour, and the spectrum of one glowing gas or vapour from that of another. If the spectrum of a glowing substance consists of bright lines or bands, the substance is certainly gaseous; if the spectrum, though continuous, has certain bands much brighter than the rest, a portion of the glowing source of light is certainly gaseous, unless the bright bands correspond to those given by the earths Erbia or Didymium; if the spectrum is continuous, and shows no band-like portions much brighter than the rest, the source of light is either a glowing solid or liquid body, or a gaseous body at very high temperature and pressure; where there is independent reason for believing that the substance forming the source of light cannot be at a very high pressure the inference is safe that it is either solid or liquid. Again, if the bright lines of an observed spectrum occupy the precise position of the bright lines of the spectrum of some known vapour, the source of light may safely be inferred to be that vapour. Or if the spectral lines of some known vapour are seen with others in the observed spectrum of a luminous body, we may infer that that vapour forms a portion of the substance of the source of light; we shall presently see how the question whether observed lines agree exactly in position with known lines can be determined more satisfactorily than by the methods of measurement described at the close of the last chapter.

Hitherto we have considered the spectra given by self-luminous bodies. We must now inquire into the spectra of bodies which reflect or transmit light received from self-luminous bodies.

As a general rule it may be stated that the same spectrum is given by light after as before reflection. Thus the spectrum of sunlight reflected from a cloud, from snow, from white paper, &c., as already mentioned, is no other than the solar spectrum, showing the dark lines just as when the sun's direct light is examined.

But coloured objects which reflect rays of certain colours more readily than other rays, to some degree modify the spectrum of the light by which they are illuminated. Thus if a piece of paper tinted with bright yellow colouring matter is illuminated by sunlight, the spectrum of the light reflected by the paper will differ from the solar spectrum in having the yellow portion relatively brighter than the rest. Owing to the impurity of most colouring substances, as well as of all the opaque colours of terrestrial objects, little importance attaches to these variations of the solar spectrum.

It is very different with the peculiarities affecting light which in passing through partially transparent solid, or liquid or vaporous substances, has undergone partial absorption.

If we examine the spectrum of sunlight which has passed through coloured glass, we find that a portion of the spectrum is wanting. Thus most red glasses transmit red, orange, and a few yellow rays, but absorb the green, blue, indigo, and violet; some, however, transmits no yellow rays, while others transmit some green and blue rays. In all cases the red colour of the transmitted light is due to the deficiency of transmitted rays belonging to the violet end of the spectrum. Green glasses sometimes transmit rays belonging to all parts of the spectrum, but there is always a relative excess of rays belonging to the green part of the spectrum. Cobalt blue glass absorbs all the red and orange rays and most of the yellow and green, but transmits the blue rays and most of the indigo and blue-violet rays. In every case the colour of glass or crystal corresponds with the portion of the spectrum most freely transmitted. Moreover, where sunlight is transmitted the dark lines of the solar spectrum are seen in the portion of the spectrum which corresponds to the transmitted light.

The absorption by coloured liquids is more distinctly selective; in fact, in a great number of cases, the absorption is such that definite dark bands and lines are

THE MICRO-SPECTROSCOPE. 51

seen in the spectrum. The method of examining absorption spectra is to suspend between the light and the slit a test-glass containing the liquid to be examined. The light received through the slit having first passed through the liquid, the characteristic absorption spectrum of the liquid is seen. In some observations of absorption spectra, however, the quantity of the colour-

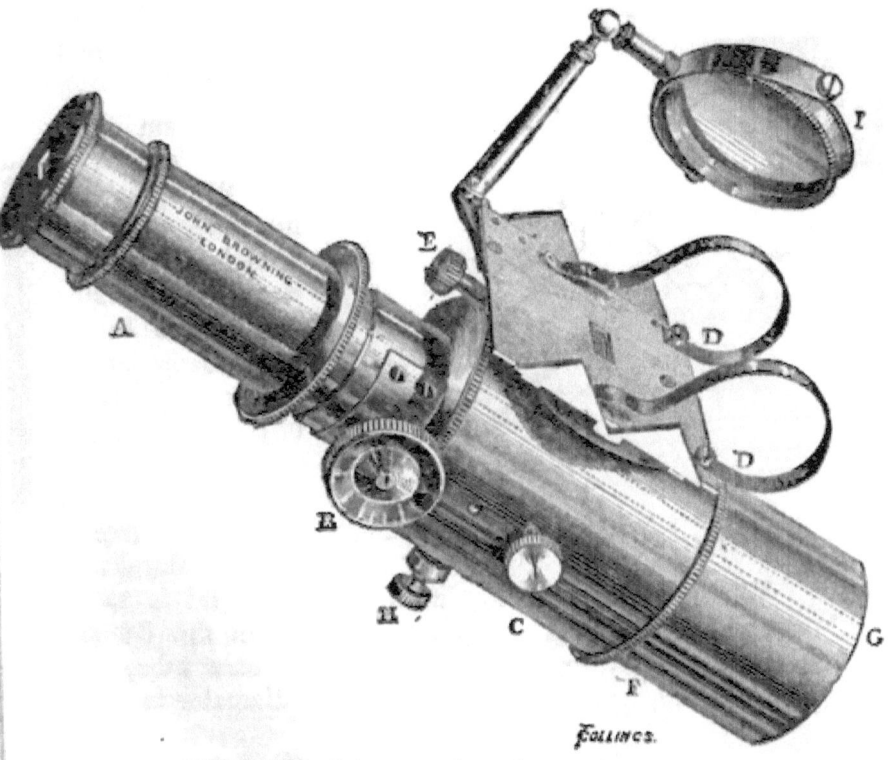

Fig. 36.—The Sorby-Browning micro-spectroscope.

ing matter at the observer's disposal is insufficient for this method, and it is necessary to use the microscope to collect light. For this purpose the micro-spectroscope has been devised by Mr. Sorby of Sheffield, who has laboured very successfully in this department of spectroscopic analysis. For the eye-piece of the microscope the instrument shown in fig. 36 is substituted. The parts lettered I, E, and D indicate the arrangements for illuminating, darkening, and adjusting an object, whose spectrum can be compared with that under examination by light received through an opening in the side of the microscope. The tube G fits into the draw-tube of the microscope, and at F is the field-glass. The spectroscopic arrangement occupies the tube A, and consists of a direct vision compound spectroscope, as shown in fig. 37, and an achromatic lens B, by which the rays are rendered parallel. The small prism close to the slit at A (fig. 37) does not interfere with the pencil of rays under examination, but serves to introduce rays from the second source of light mentioned above for comparison with those received directly through the slit.

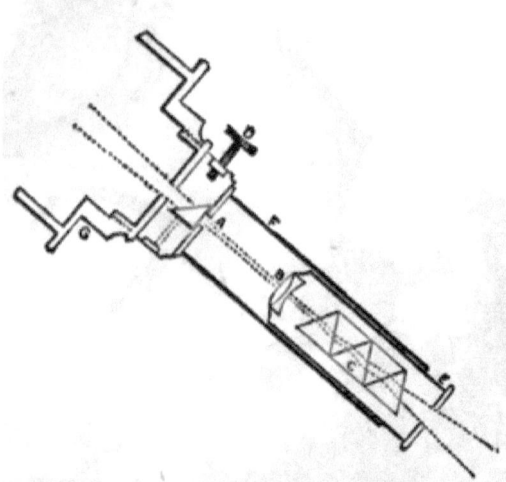

Fig. 37.—Section of the micro-spectroscope.

When a very small quantity of any fluid is to be examined, cells like the one pictured in fig. 38 are useful. They are cut from a barometer tube, and made of various depths; the interior diameter is small

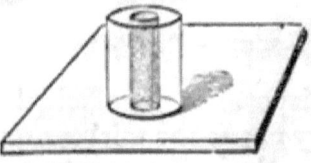

Fig. 38.—Deep cell.

Fig. 39.—Wedge cell.

enough to allow the tube to be inverted without the fluid running out. Where a varying depth of fluid is desired, to give gradation of tint, the wedge-shaped cell shown in fig. 39 may be used with advantage. Browning makes glass cells of these and other forms containing a whole series of the liquids which possess absorptive powers in any way remarkable.

Precisely as the spectra of vapours vary under varying conditions, so also do the spectra of absorbent liquids. This is well shown by the absorption spectra given by human blood. Thus we obtain four different spectra from,—(i.) fresh scarlet blood; (ii.) deoxidised blood, or cruorine; (iii.) cruorine after it has been converted by the action of an acid into hæmatine; and (iv.) deoxidised hæmatine.

Madder and the aniline dyes (magenta, mauve, aniline blue, green, red, violet, &c.), carmine, and similar substances, will be found interesting subjects for the young spectroscopist, as they possess highly characteristic absorptive powers.

Colourless gases produce no absorption bands. Coloured gases, however, exhibit bands even better defined than those produced by coloured liquids; in fact, such gases produce dark lines like the solar lines, insomuch that to examine them effectually we cannot use sunlight, for then the dark lines of sunlight would not be readily distinguishable from the dark lines belonging to the vapour we are examining. It is necessary to use the electric light or the oxyhydrogen light, producing a continuous spectrum, on which appear the dark lines or bands produced by the absorption of the coloured gas. The history of this branch of the subject is particularly interesting, because the researches made into the absorption spectra of coloured vapours led directly to the interpretation of the dark lines in the solar spectrum.

Sir D. Brewster was the first to deal systematically with this branch of research. He found that when sunlight is transmitted through the thick vapours of nitrous acid a number of new dark lines are seen, especially towards the violet end of the spectrum. He found that these lines are visible when light giving a continuous spectrum is transmitted through the gas instead of sunlight. Professor Miller thus describes the results obtained by himself and Professor Daniel: "Colourless gases in no case give additional lines, or lines differing from those of Fraunhofer. The mere presence of colour is not a security that new lines will be produced; for instance, of two vapours undistinguishable by the eye, one, bromine, gives a great number of new lines, while the other, chloride of tungsten, exhibits none. The position of the new lines has no connection with the colour of the gas; with green perchloride of manganese the new lines abound in the green of the spectrum; with red nitrous acid they increase in number and density as we approach the spectrum's blue extremity." The spectrum of the vapour of iodine contains a great number of lines in the red, orange, yellow, and green, so closely set in the green that when the slit is not very fine, or the dispersion and magnifying power considerable, they seem here to form a broad black band.

The absorption spectra, like the bright line spectra of vapours, vary with conditions of temperature and pressure. Thus Brewster found that by increasing the heat of nitrous acid the lines became stronger and new lines made their appearance, until at last the whole of the spectrum was obliterated, or, in other words, the gas was rendered entirely opaque.

The vapour of water has an absorption spectrum, that is, produces its characteristic dark lines and bands, which are readily seen in the solar spectrum when the sun is near the horizon. (See Chapter VII.)

CHAPTER IV.

INTERPRETATION OF THE SOLAR SPECTRUM.

It is singular, in the presence of what is now known respecting the solar dark lines, that none of the facts described in the preceding chapter should have suggested the real meaning of the Fraunhofer lines. We shall presently see that some of the discoveries made by Brewster, Miller, Stokes, and others, involve implicitly the solution of the mystery. Yet, as Professor Tyndall remarks, "none of these distinguished men betrayed the least knowledge of the connection between the bright bands of the metals and the dark lines of the solar spectrum. The man who came nearest to the philosophy of the subject was Ångström. In a paper translated from Poggendorff's 'Annalen' by myself, and published in 1855, he indicates that the rays which a body receives are precisely those which it can emit when rendered luminous. In another place he speaks of one of his spectra giving the general impression of a reversal of the solar spectrum. Foucault, Stokes, Thomson, and Stewart have all been very close to the discovery. For my own part, the examination of the radiation and absorption of heat by gases and vapours would have led me in 1859 to the law on which all Kirchhoff's speculations are founded, had not an accident withdrawn me from the investigation."

As far back as October, 1841, Brewster recorded the following remarks in his note-book: "I have this evening (October 28) discovered the remarkable fact, that in the combustion of nitre upon charcoal there are definite bright rays, corresponding to the double lines of A and B, and the group of lines a in the space A B. The coincidence of two yellow rays with the two deficient ones at D, with the existence of definite bright rays in the nitre flame, not only at D, but at A, a, and B, is so extraordinary, that it indicates some regular connection between the two classes of phenomena."

In 1858 and 1859, the German physicists Kirchhoff and Bunsen entered upon a series of researches, whose object was to assign the true position of the lines in the spectra of various elements. They chose for a spectrum of reference the solar spectrum, and to secure great accuracy in comparing the positions of the lines of the elements and those in the solar spectrum, they adopted a plan by which, instead of mere measurement (according to the methods described at pp. 36 and 37), a direct comparison was effected, the lines in the two spectra being seen simultaneously. The way in which this was done was as follows:—

Fig. 40 represents the adjustable slit of their spectro-

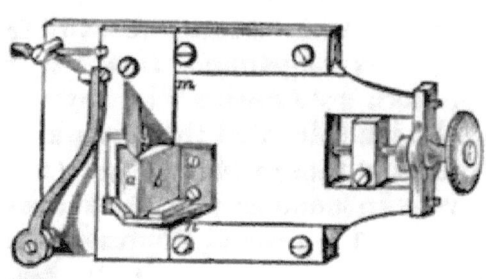

Fig. 40.—Slit used for comparing two spectra.

scope (see fig. 17, where this appendage is seen at the end of the left hand, or collimating tube). The slit is shown at mn. In front of one half is placed a small equilateral glass prism ab, which cuts off light passing directly towards the slit, but reflects through that part of the slit light received from another source. Fig. 41 shows how the prism acts. Here the light which passes directly into the slit S comes from F, while the rays from another luminous body L, after internal reflection from the face de of the prism, pass through the other half of the slit in the direction rst, or parallel to the rays from F. Thus they form a spectrum parallel to the spectrum formed by rays from L. By use of this arrangement two spectra are seen together one above the other, the upper spectrum being formed by rays which have entered the upper half of the slit directly from the source of light under analysis, while the lower spectrum is formed by rays which have entered the lower half of the slit after passing through the prism of comparison fde

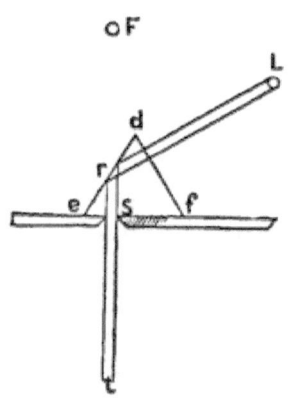

Fig. 41.—Showing the action of the prism of comparison.

(fig. 41), and being internally reflected from the face *e d*. As the rays reflected by the prism of comparison through the slit must enter in the same direction as those which pass directly into the other half of the slit, the large prism which forms the spectrum acts in precisely the same way upon rays of the same order of refrangibility from the two sources of light; so that, for instance, if the same substances are volatilised in the two flames, the lines of the lower spectrum are in exact prolongation of those of the upper spectrum. Or if the substances are unlike, then the question of the agreement or disagreement of a line in the spectrum of one with a line in the spectrum of the other can be at once determined in this way. The utility of the method for the purpose which Kirchhoff and Bunsen had in view is obvious.

Amongst other inquiries, Kirchhoff proposed to test the statement made by Fraunhofer, that the double bright orange line of the sodium spectrum (frontispiece, No. 3) agrees in position with the double dark line D of the solar spectrum. In order, says Kirchhoff, "to test in the most direct manner possible the frequently asserted fact of the coincidence of the sodium lines with the lines D, I obtained a tolerably bright solar spectrum, and brought a flame coloured by sodium vapour in front of the slit." It will be noticed that in this experiment the prism of comparison was not used; both the sunlight and the light from the sodium flame passed directly into the slit. The student may wonder, perhaps, how this could be arranged, when Kirchhoff's instrument did not permit of the collimating tube being otherwise than horizontal. The sun's rays, however, were caused by means of a movable mirror, called a heliostat, to pass horizontally into this tube throughout the experiments, at least when actual sunlight was wanted. For some purposes the light from the sky would suffice to give a sufficiently bright solar spectrum. In the experiment now in question the spectrum was not full sunlight.

It will be clear, further, that if Fraunhofer's statement was correct, then, since the bright lines given by the sodium flame would fall upon the very place occupied by the dark solar lines D, these would either not be so dark, or might even be replaced by bright lines, according as the brightness of the lines from the sodium flame fell somewhat short of, or somewhat exceeded, the brightness of the solar spectrum. The latter was the case. "I saw the dark lines D change," says Kirchhoff, "into bright ones." The accuracy of Fraunhofer's statement was thus established. Finding, however, that the flame of a Bunsen's lamp in this experiment threw the bright sodium lines upon the solar spectrum with unexpected brilliancy, Kirchhoff determined to ascertain how far "the intensity of the solar spectrum could be reduced without impairing the distinctness of the sodium lines." He therefore allowed the full sunlight to shine through the sodium flame. "To my astonishment," he says, "I saw that the dark lines D appeared with an extraordinary degree of clearness"—that is to say, it was darker than usual, or than the other lines in the spectrum. When we remember that the light from the sodium flame fell precisely upon the solar dark lines D, we can understand Kirchhoff's astonishment at the lines appearing darker than before. It was as though an experimenter had thrown a beam of light exactly upon a shadow, and had seen the shadow made darker and more distinct, instead of fainter.

In order to test this strange result, Kirchhoff "exchanged," he tells us, "the sun's light for the Drummond, or oxyhydrogen lime-light, which, like that of all incandescent solid or liquid bodies, gives a spectrum containing no dark lines. When this light was allowed to fall through a suitable flame, coloured by common salt, dark lines were seen in the spectrum in the position of the sodium lines. The same phenomenon was observed if, instead of the incandescent line, a platinum wire was used, which, being heated in

INTERPRETATION OF THE SOLAR DARK LINES. 59

a flame, was brought to a temperature near its melting point by passing an electric current through it."

This experiment was even more remarkable than the preceding. For now Kirchhoff *seemed* to have obtained darkness by combining two lights. The electric or oxyhydrogen light alone covered with its continuous spectrum the place where the sodium lines appear in the solar spectrum; the sodium flame alone lit up this part of the spectrum. When both were shining together, it was to be expected that this part of the spectrum would be brighter than the rest; but instead of that there seemed to result darkness. In reality there was only relative, not absolute darkness, the place where the dark lines appeared being really illuminated as brightly as if the sodium flame alone were shining; but by contrast with the bright continuous spectrum of the electric light, or of the oxyhydrogen flame, this faint illumination appeared as darkness. In this experiment the sodium flame acted the part of an absorbing vapour. There was nothing new or surprising in the fact that glowing vapour should absorb light. The important point was, that the rays which the sodium flame absorbed corresponded precisely with the rays which the flame emitted. Or, remembering that the emission of light from a body results from a vibratory motion of the ultimate particles of the body, it appeared from this experiment that those special vibratory motions which occur in glowing sodium vapour receive without transmitting (that is to say, *absorb*) the corresponding vibratory motions proceeding from the sun, the electric spark, or the oxyhydrogen flame. These special rays falling on the sodium flame, and absorbed by it, tend necessarily to heat it, but the heat so excited is parted with as fast as received (or appreciably so), the result being that the sodium flame continues effectually to absorb all those rays falling upon it which correspond to the light which it emits itself.

Kirchhoff experimented on other elements. He found that glowing potassium vapour causes absorption lines to appear on the continuous spectrum of the limelight, these lines corresponding precisely in position with the bright lines in the spectrum of the potassium flame viewed alone. Kirchhoff and Bunsen working together established the same law for the spectra of lithium, calcium, strontium, and barium. By these and other researches the general law has been established, that "every substance which emits at a given temperature rays of certain orders of refrangibility, possesses the power at that same temperature of absorbing rays of those same orders of refrangibility."

But now consider what interesting meaning was given to the solar dark lines by this discovery! Kirchhoff had proved that when the electric light shines through glowing sodium vapour, the sodium dark lines appear on the continuous spectrum of the electric light. It is obvious, then, that sunlight also, which shows the sodium dark lines, must before reaching us have passed through the vapour of sodium. And the other dark lines in the solar spectrum, are they not just as obviously due to absorption exercised by other vapours through which the sun's rays have passed? Either in our own atmosphere, or in the atmosphere of the sun, vapours must exist, of which sodium is certainly one, which cause these dark lines to appear in the solar spectrum. Kirchhoff's next labour was to determine what other vapours, besides sodium, thus intercept portions of the light originally emitted by the sun, and to show in passing that it must be in the sun's atmosphere, not in our own, that these vapours exist.

In these researches he made use of the prism of comparison illustrated in figs. 40 and 41. He compared the spectra of a number of terrestrial elements with that of the sun. Among the first, he took the spectrum of iron, which, as known to him, contained sixty-five bright lines, but really contains more than 450. This was a spectrum, then, very unlike the simple spectrum of sodium. But it gave evidence of precisely the same kind, only still more effective.

Every one of the iron bright lines had its counterpart in the spectrum of the sun. Line for line, strong line for strong line, and faint line for faint line, every line of the iron spectrum appears as a dark line in the spectrum of the sun. The nature of the evidence is illustrated by fig. 42, which shows a part of the double spectra of

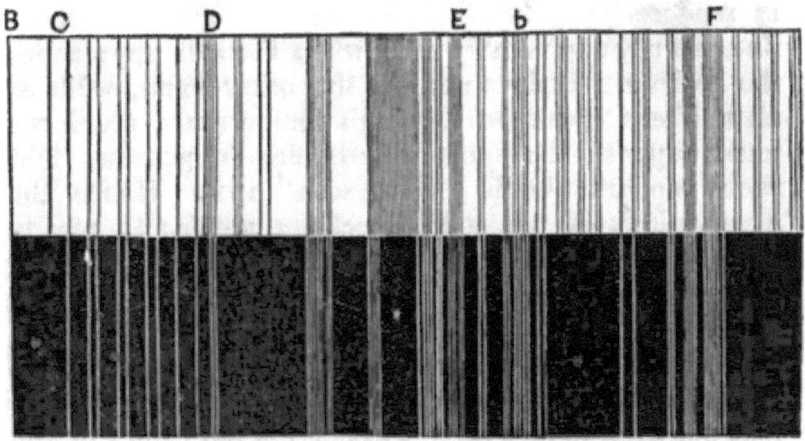

Fig. 42.—Coincidence of the lines of iron with the Fraunhofer lines. (The bright lines are only a few of the known iron lines.)

the sun (the uppermost), and of iron (the lowermost). It will be seen at once that the evidence in the case of the iron lines is altogether irresistible. Kirchhoff, treating the matter as a problem of probabilities, and taking the chance of an agreement of a dark solar line with any given line of iron at $\frac{1}{2}$, deduced for the odds against the observed coincidence the tremendous value 1,000,000,000,000 to 1.

"Hence," he reasoned, "this coincidence must be produced by some cause, and a cause can be assigned which affords a perfect explanation of the phenomenon. The observed phenomenon may be explained by the supposition that the rays of light which form the solar spectrum have passed through the vapour of iron, and have thus suffered the absorption which the vapour of iron must exert. As this is the only assignable cause of the coincidence, the supposition appears to be a necessary one. These iron vapours might be sustained either in the atmosphere of the sun or in that of the earth. But it is not easy to understand how our atmosphere can contain such a quantity of iron vapour as would produce the very distinct absorption lines which we see in the solar spectrum; and this supposition is rendered still less probable by the fact that these lines do not appreciably alter when the sun approaches the horizon. It does not, on the other hand, seem at all unlikely, owing to the high temperature which we must suppose the sun's atmosphere to possess, that such vapours should be present in it. Hence the observations of the solar spectrum appear to me to prove the presence of iron vapour in the solar atmosphere with as great a degree of certainty as we can attain in any question of natural science." It may be added to Kirchhoff's reasoning here that the evidence obtained respecting the spectra of stars suffices to show that our atmosphere cannot cause the dark lines of the solar spectrum. For if this were so, the spectrum of each star should show the same dark lines, which is not the case.

Continuing his researches, Kirchhoff found that calcium, magnesium, and chromium exist in the solar atmosphere. The presence of nickel and cobalt seemed to be indicated by the agreement of their most conspicuous lines with solar dark lines. All the lines of these elements could not be recognised, however, nor could Kirchhoff satisfy himself of the existence of cobalt in the sun. "I consider myself entitled," he says, "to conclude that nickel is present in the solar atmosphere; but I do not yet express an opinion as to the presence of cobalt. Barium, copper, and zinc appear to be present in the solar atmosphere, but only in small quantities; the brightest of the lines of these metals correspond to distinct lines in the solar spectrum, but the weaker lines are not noticeable. The remaining metals which I have examined, viz., gold, silver, mercury, aluminium, cadmium, tin, lead, antimony, arsenic, strontium, and lithium, are, according to my observations, not visible in the solar atmosphere."

Later researches by methods based on Kirchhoff's great discovery have shown that the sun's atmosphere contains the glowing vapours of the elements named in the following table, which also indicates the number of Fraunhofer lines corresponding with bright lines in the spectra of these several elements:—

Hydrogen	4	Manganese	57
Sodium	9	Chromium	18
Barium	11	Cobalt	19
Calcium	75	Nickel	33
Magnesium	$4 + (3?)$	Zinc	2
Aluminium	2?	Copper	7
Iron	450	Titanium	200
	Cadmium	?	

It is not to be inferred that because other elements have not been identified by this method they therefore do not exist in the solar atmosphere. It is manifest that for an element to attest its presence in this way, it must not only be present in considerable relative quantity, but in such a condition as to rise above the lower strata of the sun's atmosphere to regions where a relatively lower temperature prevails. For vapours can only exercise absorption on the rays from any luminous body when cooler than that body; and thus there might be enormous masses of vapour deep down in the solar atmosphere giving no spectroscopic signs of their presence, because so intensely heated. It seems probable, indeed, that the sun contains all the terrestrial elements, and possibly in proportions not differing very greatly from those that prevail in our own earth.

Although Kirchhoff's speculations concerning the sun's condition cannot be compared in value with his observational researches, they may be considered here with advantage. He supposes the sun to consist of a solid or partially liquid nucleus in a state of intense heat, emitting therefore rays of all orders of refrangibility.

Around this nucleus is an exceedingly complex atmosphere of comparatively low temperature, containing the vapours of many of the elements forming the sun's body. The rays of light emitted by the nucleus are partially absorbed by the vapours in the sun's atmosphere, each vapour absorbing rays such as it emits at the same temperature, and so causing dark lines agreeing in position with the bright lines of its spectrum as a glowing gas.

The part of Kirchhoff's theory which is certainly true is that relating to the vapours in the solar atmosphere. It is impossible to question their existence, and that they must be cooler than the substances giving the bright portions of the spectrum. But it is not by any means certain that the great mass of the sun consists of solid or liquid matter. We have seen that, even at the pressures and temperatures which can be obtained in terrestrial experiments, some of the vapours give continuous spectra, and it seems certain that at the enormous pressures and temperatures prevailing throughout the greater portion of the sun's globe most vapours would give such spectra. Even if most of the vaporous constituents of the *deeper* parts of the solar atmosphere gave only broad-band spectra, yet from a combination of many such spectra a continuous spectrum would necessarily result. From what we know about the sun, his small mean density (less than a fourth of the earth's) and the mobility of his visible parts to a great depth (where enormous pressure must exist), there seem to be good reasons for believing that all the light which forms the continuous background of the solar spectrum comes from gaseous matter at great pressure.

Let us now inquire how the new methods of research depending on Kirchhoff's discovery have been applied to other problems connected with the sun. In the first place, however, it will be well to enunciate the general laws of spectroscopic analysis as they result from the facts described in the last chapter so soon as Kirchhoff's discovery had shown the real relation between spectra of emission and of absorption. They are as follows :—

1. An incandescent solid or liquid body gives a continuous spectrum.

2. A glowing vapour gives a spectrum of bright lines or bands, each vapour having, between given limits of temperature and pressure, its characteristic set of bright lines or bands. But some vapours (and probably all) at very high temperature and pressure give continuous spectra. When a spectrum of bright lines or bands agrees with the known spectrum of a vapour between known limits of temperature, we may infer that the source of light is that vapour, and that the temperature of the vapour lies between those limits. A similar inference may be drawn when a spectrum shows the lines or bands belonging to two or more vapours.

3. An incandescent solid or liquid body, shining through absorbent vapours, gives a continuous spectrum crossed by dark lines or bands, these lines or bands having the same position as the bright lines or bands belonging to the spectra of those vapours at the same temperature and pressure; so that the nature of the absorbent vapours producing such dark lines or bands may be inferred, precisely as the nature of glowing vapours may be inferred from their bright-line spectra. Absorbent vapours, also, existing at such temperatures as not to be luminous, so that their bright-line spectra are not known, may be identified by their characteristic dark bands.

4. Probably glowing vapours at very high temperature and pressure shining through cooler absorbent vapours give the same spectrum as incandescent solid or liquid bodies shining through the same vapours.

5. Light reflected from an opaque body gives the same spectrum as it would have given before reflection from that body, but fainter. If the body is coloured, those parts of the reflected spectrum will be relatively stronger which are most freely reflected by the body.

6. If an opaque body be surrounded by a vapour or

vapours, the spectrum of light reflected from the body will be crossed by the characteristic dark lines of the vapour or vapours. So also light refracted through absorbent media, or which has passed through such media in any way, shows the spectrum which it would have given before falling on the media, but with the dark lines or bands due to the media superadded.

7. If a reflecting body is itself luminous, the spectrum belonging to it is combined with the spectrum belonging to the reflected light.

8. Glowing vapours surrounding an incandescent body will cause bright or dark lines to appear in the spectrum according as they are at a higher or lower temperature than the body; if they are at the same temperature they will emit just so much light as to compensate for that which they absorb, in which case there will remain no trace of their presence.

9. The electric spark presents a bright-line spectrum compounded of the spectra belonging to those vapours between which, and of those through which, the discharge takes place. The relative intensities of the component parts of the spectrum will depend on the nature of these vapours and of the discharge itself.

In the observations which had thus far been made upon the solar spectrum, the light analysed had come from the whole disc of the sun. For, rays from all parts of the disc passed in through the slit and fell upon the collimating lens. But it is possible to examine the spectrum of particular portions of the sun, if, instead of allowing the rays from the whole disc to fall on the slit, only the rays from a definite part of the sun are suffered so to fall. This can be effected by using a telescope. If we direct an astronomical telescope towards the sun an image of the sun is found at the focus of the object-glass; and if the slit occupied that position only, the light belonging to a portion of the sun's image equal in extent to the size of the slit, could pass in for analysis. This is illustrated in fig. 43, where the circle S represents the solar image, and the fine line of light s s' represents the portion of this image which is received through the slit. Now, what the spectroscope really does, is to give us a range of pictures of whatever luminous object, or part of an object, would be visible through the slit if the spectroscope were removed. Supposing, then, such a portion of the solar photosphere were observed as is shown within s s' (fig. 43), the images of this portion will form

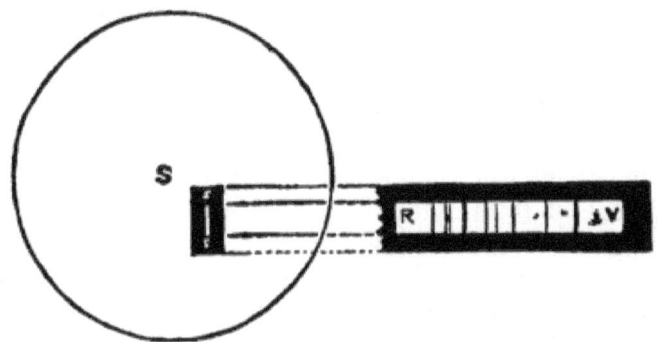

Fig. 43.—Illustrating the spectroscopic analysis of the sun's surface.

such a spectrum as R V, showing the dark lines due to the vapours above that portion s s' of the sun's surface, no other portion of the sun's disc producing any effect whatever. Thus, by means of this arrangement we can ascertain whether the various parts of the solar disc give the same spectrum. We can examine successively the brighter central parts, the darker parts near the edge, the brilliant faculæ, the spots larger or smaller, and whatever other features of the solar surface seem best to deserve attention.

To illustrate the method in which such inquiries are pursued, let us suppose that the space s s of fig. 43 falls athwart a solar spot in the manner illustrated in the left hand view of fig. 44. Then the portion of the sun's surface under spectroscopic scrutiny is that shown

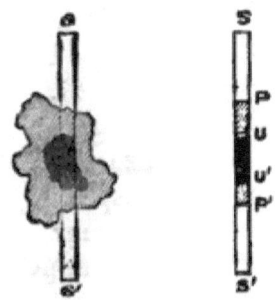

Fig. 44. — Spectroscopic analysis of a sun spot.

within the slit S S' in the right hand figure. The spectrum of this portion will consist of a number of images of S S' ranged side by side, so as to form such a strip as R V in fig. 43: at the top and bottom of this spectrum there will be two narrow solar spectra corresponding to the parts S P and S' P'; next to these will be two narrow spectra of the penumbral parts of the spot, P U and P' U'; and in the middle there will be a narrow spectrum corresponding to the umbral part U U'; all these spectra forming one compound spectrum.

The first to apply this method to the solar spots was Mr. Lockyer, who, in 1866, discovered that the spectrum of the dark parts of spots is the same in general as the spectrum of the brighter portions of the sun's surface, but fainter, showing that the darkness is in the main due to general absorption (or feebler emission on account of reduced temperature). And as the darker parts of the spots give the fainter portions of the spectra, it is clear that the absorption (or the enfeeblement of *emission*) is proportioned to the apparent darkness of the spots. Thus the cause of the darkness of the spots is shown *not* to be, as was supposed by some continental astronomers, the vaporisation of the matter of the solar photosphere, but either the interposition of relatively cool matter exercising a general absorption, or else a cooling of portions of the photosphere. But besides the enfeeblement of the solar spectrum, where there is a spot, there are signs also of increased absorption by some of the vapours which cause the dark lines. Thus the D lines are notably widened, in the manner illustrated (in the case of a hydrogen line) farther on, fig. 67, p. 120. This result has been confirmed by Secchi, Huggins, and Young.

The examination of detailed portions of the sun's surface, especially in the neighbourhood of spots, has shown further that the hydrogen lines are variable, sometimes appearing darker and wider than usual, sometimes showing bright instead of dark, at other times disappearing by becoming of the same brightness as the neighbouring parts of the spectrum. Where a facula forms part of the section under examination, the hydrogen line commonly appears bright. We thus learn that the glowing hydrogen, which forms an important constituent of the solar atmosphere, is not always or everywhere at the same temperature and pressure.

This leads us to consider one of the most interesting applications of spectroscopic analysis which has yet been effected—the study, viz., of objects seen outside the sun's globe during total solar eclipses, or, in other words, the study of those exterior and less luminous parts of the sun's globe which cannot ordinarily be seen.

CHAPTER V.

THE SOLAR PROMINENCES, CORONA, ETC.

DURING total solar eclipses there are seen around the black body of the eclipsing moon red objects, which are called the coloured prominences. They are now known not to be real prominences, but the name, as corresponding to their appearance, is still retained. During the eclipse of 1851 it was proved that these objects belong to the sun, not, as some had suggested, to the moon; for the body of the moon was seen to traverse them. Any doubts which may still have remained were disposed of by the photographs which De la Rue and Secchi obtained during the eclipse of 1860 in Spain. The two views, for instance, forming figs. 45 and 46,

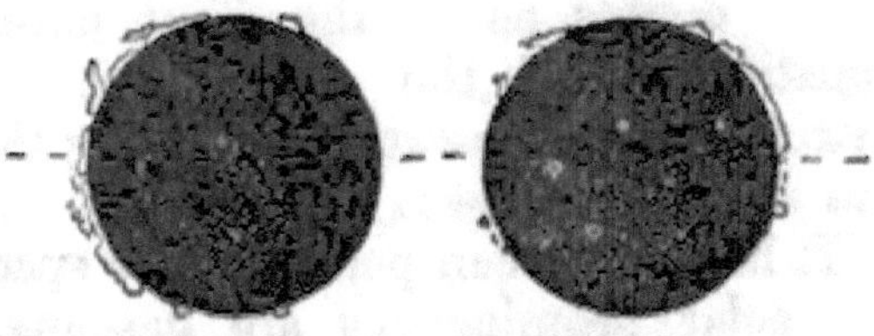

Fig. 45. Fig. 46.

From photographs of the total eclipse of June, 1860 (*De la Rue*).

represent two photographs taken by M. De la Rue, (1)

near the beginning, (2) near the end of totality; and it is clearly seen that the moon has traversed the prominences during the interval between these instants. From the observed dimensions of some of these solar appendages it was seen that they extend to a distance of 80,000, and even 100,000, miles from the sun's surface. But their real nature remained unknown until the spectroscope was applied to them during the Indian eclipse of August, 1868.

On that occasion Capt. J. Herschel, Col. Tennant, M. Janssen, and M. Rayet, succeeded in seeing the spectrum of the prominences, and found it to consist of bright lines. Herschel saw three lines—red, orange, and blue—which he associated with the Fraunhofer lines, C, D, and F. Tennant saw five, which he associated with the lines C, D, b, F, and G of the solar spectrum. Janssen saw six—red, yellow, green (two), blue, and violet—and he associated the red and blue lines with C and F of the solar spectrum. Rayet saw nine lines, the five brightest of which he associated with the Fraunhofer lines, B, D, E, b, and F.

It was proved thus that the prominences are masses of glowing vapour, and rendered almost certain that hydrogen is one of the chief constituents of these vapour masses. It seemed not improbable that another constituent was the glowing vapour of sodium.

But almost immediately on this discovery followed another of greater importance, which not only disposed of all doubts as to the exact nature of the gaseous constituents of the prominences, but also afforded astronomers the means of studying these objects without the aid of an eclipse.

It had long been perceived by spectroscopists that, if the solar prominences are gaseous, the spectroscope should afford the means of indicating their presence when the sun is not eclipsed. Stone, Lockyer, Secchi, and Huggins had all thought of this, though only Lockyer and Huggins had enunciated the idea publicly—

Lockyer, somewhat vaguely,* in October, 1866, Huggins definitely in February, 1868. The principle of the method is sufficiently simple. In ordinary telescopic observation of the sun the prominences are completely obliterated from view by the contrivance used to reduce the light of the sun so that the eye can bear it. Nor can the prominences be seen even though direct sunlight is excluded, because of the illumination of our air all around and over the sun's place in the heavens. But when the sun's light and the light of the illuminated air are dispersed by means of a spectroscope, the light of the prominences is not similarly dispersed. For suppose PP′ (fig. 47), is a prominence, S S′ the edge of the sun, and ss' the space included by the slit. Then from the portion pp' we receive the light of the prominence, and also that of our own air, illuminated by the sun's rays, the latter part of the light preventing us from discerning the former. But when the spectroscope is used, the light from the illuminated air (being sunlight) is dispersed into the solar spectrum R V, fainter than the adjacent spectrum below formed by the light from $p's'$, on the sun's edge. The light from the prominence is dispersed into the bright lines at C and F, and near D. It is not like the light from the air spread over a large space R V, but simply separated into these lines. If we increase the dispersion we make the spectrum R V fainter, but only throw the bright prominence lines farther apart. Hence, if we only have enough dispersive power we can make sure of rendering the prominence lines visible.

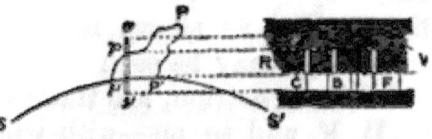

Fig. 47.—Illustrating the spectroscopic method of observing prominences.

* His words were these: "May not the spectroscope afford us evidence of the existence of the 'red flames' which total eclipses have revealed to us in the sun's atmosphere, although they escape all other methods of observation at other times?" Huggins, in point of fact, answered this question by stating definitely, in February, 1868, how this might be done.

Janssen succeeded in applying this method the day following the eclipse of 1868. But the news of his success did not reach Europe for two months, and a day or two before it arrived Mr. Lockyer had obtained similar success. In fact, when once the gaseity of the prominences and the position of the bright lines had been indicated (by Herschel, Rayet, Tennant, and Janssen), it had become easy to see the bright lines with the spectroscope, as was shown by Janssen's success on the day immediately following the eclipse.

The new method of observing the prominence spectrum enabled the observer to determine at his leisure, and very exactly, the true position of the prominence lines. For, as shown in fig. 47, the spectrum of the sun's edge may be seen at the same time, and *there*, in the solar spectrum, are those very lines—the dark lines, C, D, F, and so on—with which the eclipse observers had associated the prominence bright lines. It is only necessary to see whether those dark lines agree in position with the bright ones, to tell whether the prominence lines are due, or not, to the presence of those particular elements which produce such solar lines. It will be understood that, in applying this method, the whole of the spectrum is not seen at once, but only a small portion. It is easy, therefore, to perceive the necessity for an automatic arrangement like that illustrated in fig. 18, by means of which the adjustment of the spectroscope for every part of the prism is effected by the same movement which brings each part successively into view.

Janssen found in this way that the red and blue prominence lines coincide with the lines C and F; so that the prominences consist in part of the glowing vapour of hydrogen. He found, however, that the orange line does not correspond, as had been supposed, with the sodium double line D. By the new method other lines could be recognised. Fig. 48 shows the prominence spectrum of bright lines, and the adjacent solar spectrum as seen by Mr. Lockyer. It will be seen that of the five strongest lines, four correspond with strong

solar lines, C, F, G, and H, while the fifth is close to
the double sodium line D. It will be noticed that there
are shorter lines, of which one pair corresponds with the

Fig. 48.—The spectrum of a prominence.

D lines, while three correspond with the group *b* (magnesium), showing that in the prominence under examination there were the vapours of sodium and magnesium, but not reaching to the same height as the hydrogen. It will be observed also that one of the magnesium lines is shorter than the other, as though the upper portions of the magnesium vapour in the prominence gave a simpler spectrum than the lower—two lines instead of three—in consequence of diminished pressure and temperature. The F line of hydrogen is seen to widen as it approaches the solar spectrum, corresponding to an increase of pressure and temperature in the lower parts of the prominence, to which the widened part of the line belongs.

Careful examination showed that the bright lines can be obtained at all parts of the sun's edge, though reaching only to a short distance from the edge where there is no prominence. This layer of prominence matter (glowing hydrogen and other vapours) surrounding the visible globe of the sun, is sometimes called the *sierra*, sometimes the *chromosphere*. The former name agrees well with the name given to the prominences; and as it was given by those who first observed this layer, it seems preferable to the awkward word chromosphere (which is also incorrectly formed).*

* It should have been *chromatosphere*, chromosphere being in fact as incorrect as ' chromic ' would be for chromatic, or ' chronatic ' for chronic.

It will easily be seen from fig. 47 that the shape of a prominence can be determined by this method of observation. Thus the recognition of any one of the bright lines in the spectrum R V of fig. 47 shows that at p' on the sun's edge prominence matter reaches as high as p, and by shifting the place of the slit from p' to P' the shape of the prominence above that arc of the sun's edge can be ascertained. We can also get any number of cross sections of a prominence in other directions. For instance, if S S' (fig. 49) is a part of the sun's edge, P P' a prominence, we can get from such a strip as $s s'$ the spectrum R V, and by combining a number of strips taken parallel to $s s'$ we can learn the true shape of the prominence P P'.

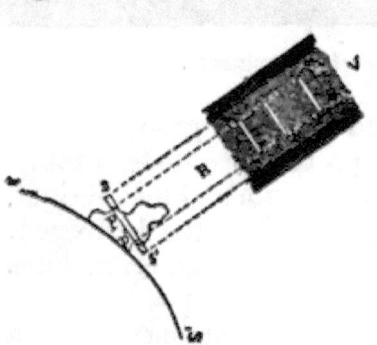

Fig. 49.—Spectroscopic method of observing thwart sections of a prominence.

But Mr. Huggins showed early in 1869, that by using sufficient dispersive power the whole of a prominence (of moderate extent) could be seen at once. If we remember that the essential object of narrowing the slit is to keep apart the images which would otherwise overlap, it will be seen that, so far as the spectrum of the prominences is concerned, a narrow slit is not required. In fact if we were examining a prominence alone we could dispense altogether with a slit, if only the dispersive power of the spectroscope were sufficient to separate from each other the images corresponding to the red, orange, and green parts of the prominence light. But since, when the sun is not eclipsed, there is the light from our own air over the prominence, we must in some way limit the amount of this light which reaches the eye. We can then only open the slit to such an extent as the dispersive power of the spectroscope will permit. Suppose, for instance, that instead of a narrow slit, such as $s s'$ in figs. 47 and 49, we have an open slit, as S P S' in fig. 50, and use a spectroscope of greater dispersive power forming R V, the continuous spectrum of the atmospheric illumination received through the wide slit. Then if there is a prominence as P P' within

Fig. 50.—Illustrating Huggins's method of observing an entire prominence by means of the spectroscope.

the space enclosed by the open slit, a red, an orange, and a blue-green image of the prominence will be formed at corresponding parts of the spectrum R V. Now the brightness of the continuous spectrum R V will be greater in proportion as the opening of the slit is greater, but will be diminished in proportion as the dispersive power of the spectroscope—and therefore the length of the spectrum—is increased. Thus by increasing the dispersive power, the brightness of the continuous spectrum R V may be sufficiently reduced to allow the images of the prominence to be seen, not all at once, of course, but the red, orange, or blue-green image, according as the red, orange, or blue-green portion of the spectrum R V is brought into view by the motion of the telescope and the automatic battery of prisms.

Fig. 51 represents a drawing by Mr. Huggins of the first prominence ever seen by this method.

Improvements in the practical application of this method were gradually introduced. In fact it was chiefly for this end that automatic spectroscopes were originally devised, and arrangements planned for securing great dispersive power. Huggins, in obtaining the view pictured in fig. 51, had been obliged to sup-

Fig. 51.—First prominence seen by the open slit method.

plement the dispersive action of his instrument by using a ruby red glass while examining the red image of the prominence. But with more powerful instruments since employed, there has been no occasion thus to call absorption to the aid of dispersion.

It would interest the reader greatly if we could here consider the results which have followed from the use of this method of observation, but the subject is too wide for such a book as this, and belongs properly to treatises upon the sun. It will be easy for the reader to perceive, however, from figs. 52 and 53, what light observations of this kind throw upon the nature of the solar prominences. Fig. 52 shows a group of solar prominences, extending some 30,000 miles in height (that is, from the sun's edge). Fig. 53 shows the same group an hour later, after which interval, short though it was, the position of these masses of glowing vapour had changed remarkably—for a hair's-breadth in either drawing represents ten miles.

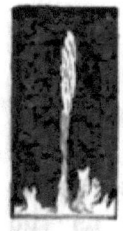
Fig. 52.
A solar prominence.

Fig. 53.
The same an hour later.

Zöllner, Young, Lockyer, Secchi, Respighi, and others have studied the solar prominences more or less systematically by this method. What they have discovered may be thus very briefly summarised. The prominences are largest and most numerous over those two zones of the sun's surface (corresponding in position to the temperate zones in our earth) where spots are seen, but are found also over the sun's polar and equatorial regions. They may be divided into two classes—eruptive prominences and cloud prominences. The former consist of glowing vapours which rush upwards with enormous velocity from the sun's surface (probably from far below that surface in reality), and after reaching a height varying from 20,000 to more than 100,000 miles, spread out laterally, subsiding gradually towards the surface, but often continuing to float for days at enormous heights. The latter class are like clouds of glowing vapour in the solar atmosphere, are often seen at a great height, rarely, however, above 80,000 miles, and change in form, but not so rapidly as the eruptive prominences. Cloud prominences alone are seen over the sun's equatorial and polar regions; they are not so bright as the eruptive prominences, and whereas these last sometimes show, besides the hydrogen lines, the lines of metallic spectra (sodium, magnesium, iron, &c.) to a great height, the cloud prominences show only the hydrogen lines and the line near D. Prominences of all kinds are few in number and attain but small dimensions when the sun shows few spots, at which time eruptive prominences are scarcely ever to be seen. Further on, we shall have to consider spectroscopic evidence of rapid motions in some of the prominences.

We have seen that low down in the prominences, sodium, magnesium, and other substances are found; and it will be understood that in the sierra, which may be regarded as simply a lower layer of prominence matter, the lines of these elements are frequently seen. Professor Young has shown that sometimes the spectrum of the sierra contains many more of these extra lines. Taking a powerful telescope to a station in the Rocky Mountains, 8,300 feet above the sea level, he has succeeded in determining the position of no less than 273 bright lines seen in the sierra spectrum. These lines indicated the presence in the sierra, or at least in its lower parts, of sodium, iron, magnesium, barium, calcium, cadmium, titanium, manganese, sulphur, cerium, strontium, and (with somewhat less probability) zinc, erbium, yttrium, lanthanum, and didymium. He also observed " some coincidences with the spectra of oxygen, nitrogen, and bromine, but not enough, considering the total number of lines in the spectra of these elements " to warrant any positive conclusion. One line seems to indicate the presence of either iridium or ruthenium.

We owe to Professor Young also another very interesting discovery. It occurred to him that it might be possible at the moment when total eclipse of the sun begins or ends to obtain the spectrum belonging to the complex vaporous atmosphere outside the sun. Under ordinary conditions, we know that the sun we see gives a rainbow-tinted spectrum crossed by lines; and we know, moreover, that the continuous rainbow-tinted spectrum comes from the glowing mass of the sun, while the dark lines are caused by the absorptive action of relatively cool vapours which surround that mass. But these vapours, though relatively cool, must in reality be intensely hot, for iron (to take one only of the vaporous constituents) is not vaporised save at an intensely high temperature. These vapours, when shining alone, then, ought to give a spectrum consisting of multitudinous bright lines—of the same lines, in fact, which, projected on the brighter background of the continuous solar spectrum, appear dark. Now when the sun was totally eclipsed in 1868 and 1869 the light from matter outside his glowing orb was not found to give these multitudinous bright lines. Hence it was clear that the complex solar atmosphere does not reach high above the surface of the sun we see—not so high certainly as the sierra, for while the light of the sierra was under examination the spectrum of thousands of bright lines had not been seen. It was still possible, however, that the spectrum of many bright lines might be seen if specially looked for at the very instant when the sun's globe is totally eclipsed, or at the very instant before it begins to reappear after eclipse. It was in fact probable (as I had myself pointed out some time before the eclipse of 1870) that the sun's complex atmosphere is very shallow, relatively to the sun's own dimensions; and this being so, its light would only shine *alone* for a second or two after totality begins, and again for a second or two before totality ends. With the object of determining whether this is the case or not, Professor Young directed a spectroscope towards the part of the sun's edge which was the last to disappear on the occasion of the total eclipse of December, 1870. So long as any portion of the sun was visible he saw the usual solar spectrum, growing fainter and fainter, however, as the sun gradually disappeared from view. At length this spectrum disappeared altogether, and then there suddenly appeared the most beautiful spectacle spectroscopic observation can afford—thousands of bright lines, the spectrum of that complex solar atmosphere which, under ordinary conditions, produces by its absorptive action the corresponding dark lines of the solar spectrum. The spectacle lasted but a few seconds; for the advancing body of the moon quickly concealed the solar atmosphere as it had already concealed the solar globe; but just before the solar globe reappeared, the atmosphere was again in view, without direct sunlight, for a few seconds; and during that time the beautiful spectrum of multitudinous bright lines of all the colours of the rainbow (ranged too in rainbow sequence) was again seen.

Outside the solar prominences there can be seen during total eclipse the solar corona, a glory of light extending sometimes to a distance from the sun exceeding his apparent diameter. Its ordinary appearance is represented in fig. 54, but sometimes it shows curiously curved streaks of light, such as are depicted in fig. 55.* The corona presents phenomena which, when carefully studied, show that its light comes from matter surrounding the sun; yet doubts were entertained for a long time upon this point (the force of the evidence being only evident to mathematicians); and it was not until the easily understood evidence of eclipse-photographs had been obtained, that the

* The light of the corona is usually too delicate for observers to recognise such details. But fortunately during the eclipse of 1871 (seen in India, &c.) photographs of the corona were obtained, which present an amazing complexity of structure. A steel engraving alone can present the appearance of the corona properly. For the details shown in the photographs then obtained, see Plate IX. of the author's "Treatise on the Sun."

generality perceived that the corona is a solar appendage. The spectroscope gave valuable evidence on this point, but it will save time to consider the spectroscopic

Fig. 54.—The solar corona (eclipse of 1842).

results apart from a question which is now definitely disposed of.

During the eclipse of 1869, observed in America, it was found that while a portion of the coronal light gives a faint continuous spectrum, in which the American observers could distinguish no dark lines, another portion gives a spectrum consisting of one bright green line (two other lines were seen which probably belonged to the light from the prominences). The bright line was identified by Professor Young with a line of iron (numbered 1474 of Kirchhoff's scale), and much perplexity was occasioned by the questions thus suggested. How came it, for instance, that one line only of the many lines belonging to the spectrum of iron was visible? And, again, under what conditions could iron exist, at this great distance from the sun, in the form of glowing vapour? These difficulties have since been removed by Young's discovery that the corona line,

Fig. 55.—The solar corona, (eclipse of 1858, *Liais*).

though very close to the iron line 1474, is not absolutely identical with it in position.

During the eclipse of December, 1870, the results obtained in 1869 were in general respects confirmed. But Denza, an Italian observer, saw two bright lines in the spectrum of the corona, a fact suggesting the probability that the corona may be variable.

During the eclipse of December, 1871, Respighi observed that the bright lines of the corona are obtained from matter more than 200,000 miles from the surface of the sun; for, using a battery of prisms without any slit, he saw three coloured spectral images of the corona extending to that distance from the sun. Two of these images were due to glowing hydrogen, the third to the line near 1474. On this occasion Janssen showed that, besides the 1474 line and the lines of hydrogen, several fainter lines exist in the gaseous spectrum of the corona. But he made a still more important discovery in noting that the solar dark lines can be recognised on the faint continuous spectrum of the corona. For this showed that besides the gaseous matter of the corona there must be matter capable of reflecting sunlight. It may reasonably be inferred that this matter is simply the more condensed part of the meteoric dust which surrounds the sun on all sides, but more densely near the plane in or close to which the planets travel.

It appears that the zodiacal light, which is probably due to this same meteoric dust, gives also a faint continuous spectrum, in which probably the dark solar lines might be recognised were it not for the exceeding faintness of the spectrum and the consequent necessity of using a wide slit. Some observers had supposed the spectrum of the zodiacal light to consist of the same bright lines which form the spectrum of the aurora borealis; but it appears from the observations of Professor Piazzi Smyth that this is not the case. Those bright lines (see Chapter VII.) are sometimes seen in the spectrum of the diffused light from all parts of the sky, and may thus have been mistakenly regarded as belonging to the spectrum of the zodiacal light. But the true spectrum of this strange luminosity is continuous.

CHAPTER VI.

SPECTRA OF THE STARS, THE MOON, PLANETS, COMETS, ETC.

So soon as the real meaning of the solar spectrum had been ascertained, astronomers turned with renewed interest to the study of the spectra of the stars, planets, and other celestial bodies. We have already seen that the stars give spectra resembling in general features the spectrum of the sun, but differing in special details. Kirchhoff's discovery, therefore, respecting the solar spectrum related in general respects to the stars also. It showed that the stars resemble our sun, in being masses glowing with intense heat, and thus giving out light whose spectrum is continuous; while around these masses there are envelopes of vapour relatively cool, and thus absorbing certain portions of the light from the glowing mass within, so that the stellar spectrum is crossed by dark lines. Thus, when the inquiry into stellar spectra was resumed, its object was not to determine whether the stars are suns or not, for so much was already known, but to determine what manner of suns they may be; to classify them into their various orders, if such orders exist; and to ascertain what changes, if any, their light may undergo.

The first to distinguish various orders among the stars (to prove, in point of fact, that " one star differeth from another in glory ") was Dr. Louis Rutherfurd, of New York. He found that certain stars closely resemble our sun, so far as their spectra are concerned; that others, including Sirius and some of the brightest stars, are distinguished by the remarkable strength and breadth of the hydrogen dark lines; and that others have spectra characterised by broad bands.

Later, Fr. Secchi, in Italy, took up the inquiry, observing a great number of stars, and noting details of their spectra which were apparently not within the range of Rutherfurd's spectroscope. At the same time Huggins and Miller, in England, were pursuing a series of still more exact observations for the determination of the elements existing in the vaporous atmosphere of some of the brighter stars. The results obtained by Secchi are more general than those obtained by Huggins and Miller; but these last are in reality more important, and must be first considered.

It should be premised that the image of a star at the focus of the telescopic object-glass is a small bright point, and this, if dealt with in the usual way by the spectroscope, would present simply a rainbow-tinted line, unsuited for the indication of missing colours. It is necessary, therefore, to alter the image into a line, which can be done by using a cylindrical lens. Such a lens (unlike convex or concave lenses, which make all the rays falling on them tend either more quickly or less quickly to a point) bends the rays which fall on it in such a way that they converge to two focal lines,* either of which can be made to fall upon the slit of the spectroscope. Then this line of light can be examined in the usual way. Or the linear spectrum may be first formed, and a cylindrical lens used in the telescope for examining the spectrum.† In the spectroscope used by Mr. Huggins the former arrangement was adopted. This spectroscope is illustrated in fig. 56. On the left is shown the cylindrical lens (convexo-plane, so that the visible side is flat). This is at the eye end of the large telescope, the eye-piece being of course removed. The dotted lines show where the tube comes which carries the spectroscope shown in the figure. It will be seen that this spectroscope differs little from an ordinary two-prism spectroscope. The prism of comparison will be

---

* Suppose there is a pencil of rays proceeding from the circular object-glass of a telescope to the focus F, and that in the way of this pencil, and square to its axis, we interpose a convex lens. Then the rays are brought to another point F′ on the axis of the pencil, but F′ is nearer to the object-glass than F. Now if, instead of an ordinary convex lens, a cylindrical convex lens is interposed, the course of a ray from any point of the object-glass towards F is broken; but instead of the ray being bent towards F′ on the axis of the pencil, as if round the centre of the lens, it is bent as if round the axis of the cylindrical lens, and (assuming the lenses of equal focal length) the ray passes through a point in a line through F′ parallel to the axis of the lens; continuing on, it passes through a point in a line through F at right angles to the axis of the lens. These lines through F′ and F are the focal lines of the cylindrical lens. Similar considerations apply to a concave cylindrical lens, only in this case the point F′ would be farther from the object-glass than the point F.

† Mr. Huggins, commenting on Schellen's remark that either method can be used, says that the cylindrical lens should be placed before the slit (that is, between the object-glass and the slit). Probably he found some advantage in this arrangement in practice; but theoretically, either method is correct.

seen close to the cylindrical lens. The slit is half-covered as usual by this small prism, through which the

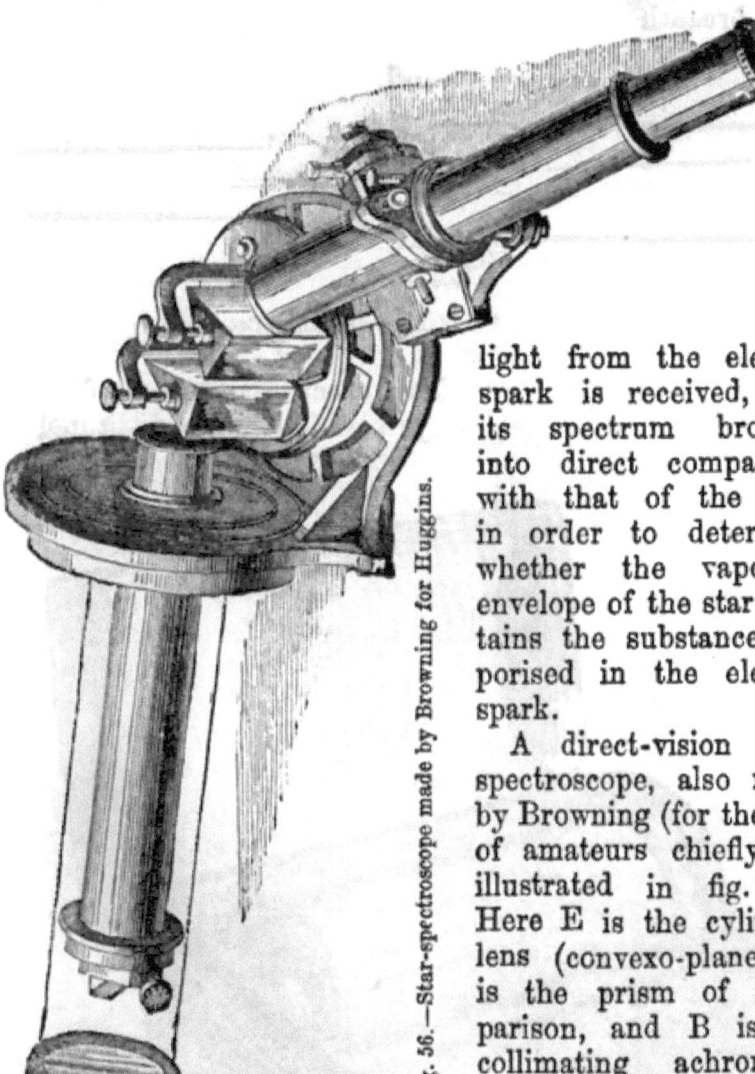

Fig. 56.—Star-spectroscope made by Browning for Huggins.

light from the electric spark is received, and its spectrum brought into direct comparison with that of the star, in order to determine whether the vaporous envelope of the star contains the substance vaporised in the electric spark.

A direct-vision star-spectroscope, also made by Browning (for the use of amateurs chiefly), is illustrated in fig. 57. Here E is the cylindric lens (convexo-plane), K is the prism of comparison, and B is the collimating achromatic lens to make the rays parallel before entering the direct-vision compound prism A.

A still more convenient arrangement is adopted in McClean's new star-spectroscope, fig. 58, by means of which exquisitely fine lines can be seen in the spectra of stars, without the use of any slit, a concave cylindrical lens (seen in the figure) being used, instead, to give breadth to the linear spectrum formed by a direct-

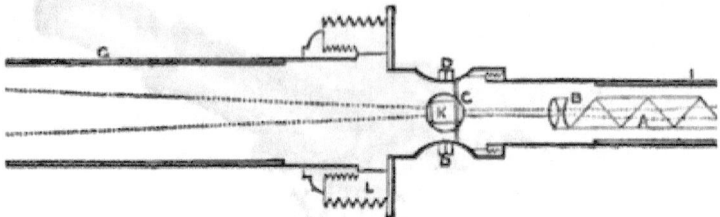

Fig. 57.—Direct-vision star-spectroscope (Browning).

vision compound prism. This spectroscope is, in fact, simply a spectroscopic eye-piece, being substituted for the ordinary eye-piece when a star-spectrum is

Fig. 58.—McClean's new star-spectroscope (Browning.)

to be examined. Mr. McClean has indeed adopted a revolving nose-piece to his own telescope, by which the change can be made instantaneously. This spectroscope is not only exceedingly simple and convenient in these respects, but as there is no occasion to keep the focal image of a star on a fine slit, the spectrum is much more easily obtained, and can be kept in view without clockwork to drive the telescope. In fact it can be used with an alt-azimuth telescope, though, of course, not so conveniently as with an equatorial.

The two stars (Aldebaran the bright red star in the head of Taurus) and Betelgeux (the brightest of the two shoulder stars of Orion) were examined very carefully by Huggins and Miller; in fact no two stars in the heavens have as yet received such careful spectroscopic analysis. As will be seen from fig. 59, about eighty lines in each spectrum were observed, and their places accurately determined by comparison with the spectral lines of several terrestrial elements. The following tables present the result of the comparison:—

TERRESTRIAL ELEMENTS COMPARED WITH ALDEBARAN.

Coincident.	Not coincident.
1. Hydrogen (lines C and F).	Nitrogen (three lines).
2. Sodium (double D line).	Cobalt (two lines).
3. Magnesium (triple b line).	Tin (five lines).
4. Calcium (four lines).	Lead (two lines).
5. Iron (E and four other lines).	Cadmium (three lines).
6. Bismuth (four lines).	Barium (two lines).
7. Tellurium (four lines).	Lithium (one line).
8. Antimony (three lines).	
9. Mercury (four lines).	

TERRESTRIAL ELEMENTS COMPARED WITH BETELGEUX.

Coincident.	Not coincident.
1. Sodium (double D line).	Hydrogen (two lines).
2. Magnesium (triple b line).	Nitrogen (three lines).
3. Calcium (four lines).	Tin (five lines).
4. Iron (E and four other lines).	Gold (?).
5. Bismuth (four lines).	Cadmium (three lines).
6. Thallium (?).	Silver (two lines).
	Mercury (two lines).
	Barium (two lines).
	Lithium (one line).

STAR-SPECTRA.

Spectrum of Aldebaran. Spectrum of Betelgeux.

Fig. 59.—Spectra of Aldebaran and Betelgeux.

We are not, of course, to infer from the absence of the known lines of any element that the element itself is absent. Especially unsafe would it be to suppose that hydrogen is absent from the vaporous envelope of Betelgeux and other stars in whose spectra the lines of hydrogen are not visible. I have already shown (p. 68) how the absence of particular lines from the spectrum of the sun may be explained, and the argument applies with much greater force to the comparatively imperfect views we obtain of the stellar spectra. Again, what we have learned about the hydrogen lines of the sun (p. 68), shows how these lines may be stronger or weaker, or evanescent, or may be changed to bright lines, in the spectrum of one and the same body.

Other stars were observed by Huggins and Miller, and presented similar results. The spectrum of Sirius is shown in the frontispiece, spectrum 10. It will be noticed that the lines of hydrogen are remarkably heavy; the presence of sodium and magnesium is also established, and the presence of iron suspected. Vega (the chief star of the Lyre) shows a similar spectrum. Capella has a spectrum resembling that of our sun, as does that of Arcturus, but not quite so closely. Both these stars show the double D line of sodium. Pollux contains sodium and magnesium, and probably iron. Procyon and Arided both show the sodium lines. Almost a hundred stars in all were examined in greater or less detail by Huggins and Miller.

Secchi, proceeding on a plan far less exact and laborious, made a wider survey, observing no less than six hundred stars. He found that the spectra of the stars which he observed could be divided into four well-marked orders.

The first order includes most of the stars which shine with a white or bluish white colour. The bright star Sirius may be taken as the type of this order (see frontispiece). It includes Sirius, Vega, Altair, Regulus, Rigel, the stars β, γ, δ, ϵ, ζ, and η of the Great Bear, the leading stars in Ophiuchus, &c. The four lines of hydrogen are remarkably strong. Besides these lines there can be seen five black lines in the yellow belonging to sodium, the chief magnesium lines, and probably some lines of iron (Secchi's method did not enable him to verify these coincidences). In the fainter stars of this order the hydrogen line C is not easily detected, the red part of the spectrum being faint. In fact, in all the stars of this type the red and yellow portions of the spectrum are much fainter than the rest. About half the stars observed by Secchi belong to this type.

The second order is that of the yellow stars, as Capella, Pollux, Aldebaran, Arcturus, Alpha of the Great Bear, Procyon, &c. The spectra of these stars closely resemble that of the sun, showing a great number of fine black lines, the strongest of which can be identified with the chief lines of the solar spectrum. It is to be noticed that all the stars classed under this type have not the same spectrum. That of Procyon, for example, is intermediate in character between the first and second types, while that of Aldebaran is intermediate between the second and third types. About one-third of the stars observed by Secchi belong to the second order.

The third order includes Betelgeux, Antares (a Scorpii), Scheat (β Pegasi), a Herculis, and others, mostly of red or orange colour. The spectrum is somewhat remarkable, consisting of a double system of nebulous bands and dark lines (see the spectrum of Betelgeux, fig. 59). The chief lines of the second type are seen, but the hydrogen lines are fainter, or not distinguishable at all. In general the spectrum of the third order resembles that of a sun spot, whence Secchi infers that these stars have spots upon them like our sun, but relatively much larger. This idea is to some degree confirmed by the fact, that among the stars of this type are some of the most remarkable variable stars. Betelgeux, for instance, is a noted irregular variable; Scheat and a Herculis are both variable; and the most wonderful (regularly) variable star in the heavens, o Ceti (justly called *Mira*), which shines as a second magnitude star for a fortnight at intervals of 330 days, taking three months in waxing from invisibility to its full magnitude and the same time in waning, belongs also to this order. It seems reasonable to infer, from the nature of their spectra, that these stars are variable in consequence of large spots upon their surface, varying in size and number like the solar spots. About thirty of the stars examined by Secchi belong to this order.

The fourth order consists of small red stars, and is characterised by a spectrum of three bright bands separated by intervening dark spaces. The brightest band lies in the green, the others in the blue and red. All these bands are brightest on the side towards the violet, where the light terminates sharply, while towards the red they fade gradually into darkness.

A fifth order may be added to Secchi's four orders. It consists of stars whose spectra show the two hydrogen lines C and F bright instead of dark. Amongst the stars of this class are γ Cassiopeiæ, β Lyræ (both variable), and the most wonderful (irregularly) variable star in the heavens, η Argûs, in which Le Sueur, using the great Melbourne telescope, saw the lines C, b, F, a line near D (the prominence line D_3), and the strongest of the nitrogen lines, as bright lines. It may be conceived that as the stars of Secchi's third type are probably covered with many and large spots, so the stars of this fifth type are covered with large facular masses, and probably with eruptive prominences.

This interpretation of spectra of the fifth class is confirmed by the appearance of the spectrum of the temporary star which blazed out in May, 1866, in the constellation of the northern crown. The spectrum of this star (called thenceforth T Coronæ),* as seen by Huggins, is represented in fig. 60. It shows clearly

---

* It must not be confounded, as in some treatises on spectrum analysis, with τ Coronæ, a star of the fifth magnitude, known to astronomers from time immemorial.

that the light of the star in its abnormal condition was of two kinds. One portion gave the usual continuous spectrum crossed by many fine lines. The other gave four bright lines (numbered 1, 2, 3, and 4 in the figure),

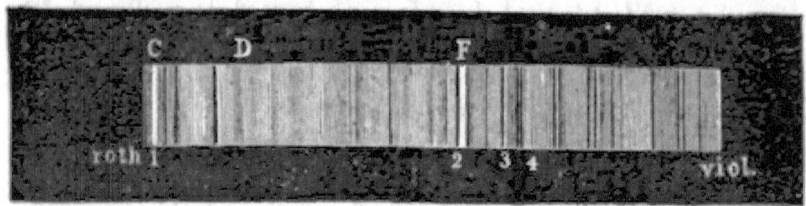

Red.   Fig. 60.—Spectrum of the temporary star T Coronæ.   Violet.

and so brilliant as to show that the greater part of the star's light was concentrated in these four lines. The line 2 was identical in position with the line F of hydrogen, and apparently the line 1 was identical with C of hydrogen. The hypothesis suggested in explanation of the spectrum and of the star's sudden increase of lustre, is that through some cause (as the downfall of a heavy mass upon T Coronæ) the star was suddenly raised to a high temperature, which caused the hydrogen surrounding the star to shine with an intense lustre, and may probably have occasioned also the outrush of enormous quantities of glowing hydrogen from beneath the star's photosphere. As the lustre of the star gradually diminished, the brightness of the four lines diminished also, the continuous spectrum also growing less lustrous. At present T Coronæ, which now shines as a star of the tenth magnitude, gives the usual spectrum of a faint star.

On November 24th, 1876, another "new" star was observed in the constellation Cygnus, or the Swan. It was detected by Professor Schmidt, of the Athens Observatory, and when first observed was shining as a third magnitude star, in a part of the constellation where no star had been visible to the naked eye, or, indeed, had been entered in any chart. It must have shone out suddenly, for Schmidt had been observing in that region on the night of November 22nd (the 23rd was cloudy). It afterwards faded gradually, though it did not entirely fade from view to the naked eye for two or three months.

The spectrum of this star was examined by M. Cornu, of the Paris Observatory. He found that, like the star T in Coronæ, it showed the bright lines of hydrogen. But besides these lines, other bright lines could be seen. One of these was an orange-yellow line, either D, or the prominence-line near D. M. Cornu was not able to determine which of these lines was really present in the star's spectrum. Another bright line, green in colour, he found to agree in position with a triple line belonging to the metal magnesium. Lastly, the bright yellowish green line was seen which is present in the spectrum of the solar corona and of the sierra.

All this agrees well with what was observed in the case of the star in the Northern Crown. For if a star increases so much in heat and lustre that the hydrogen surrounding it glows more brightly than the body of the star, then other matter outside that sun might be expected to share that increase of heat. We see that outside our own sun, besides hydrogen, a certain unknown vapour of an orange-yellow colour, magnesium, and another vapour of greenish yellow colour are present in enormous quantities. It seems, therefore, reasonable to believe that other suns have these gases extending far outside the rest of their substance. It is certain that if our sun were caused to glow with far more than its present degree of heat, the gases whose increase of brightness would be most discernible from a distant station (as a world circling around some remote star) would be precisely those gases which were glowing so resplendently around the star in the Swan, in November, 1876, or rather at the time when the light which reached us last November set out from that remote sun in Cygnus.

Another phenomenon which spectroscopic analysis has been employed to explain is the marked colour of certain stars, and especially of certain double stars. Secchi's four orders of spectra correspond, as we have seen, with the colours of the stars, and to some degree explain those colours. Certain portions of the spectrum being more or less reduced in brightness by absorption bands or lines, the light of the star is deficient in the corresponding colours, and so shows a tint resulting from the relative excess of the remaining colours. But in the case of some of the double stars, the colours are much more marked than those of any of the single stars visible to the naked eye, and it was a question of interest whether these strongly defined tints could be explained by means of the spectroscope. The result of the spectroscopic examination of the strongly coloured components—one orange, the other blue—of the fine double star Albireo, left no doubt on that point, so far at least as this star is concerned. The spectrum of the orange star shows several strong lines in the green, blue, and violet portions, and there are no lines in the orange part; thus there is an excess of orange light, and the star shines with an orange tint. In the spectrum of the smaller blue companion there are several strong bands in the orange and yellow parts of the spectrum, and very few lines elsewhere: hence there is an excess of blue and violet light, and the star shows a well marked blue colour.

STAR CLUSTERS AND NEBULÆ.

Besides the fixed stars—single, double, and multiple—the celestial depths present to us groups of stars called star clusters, which to the naked eye appear as faint clouds of light, and nebulæ, or clouds of light which are either only resolved into stars by the use of very powerful telescopes or have proved thus far altogether irresolvable.

Star clusters give in general the same spectrum as faint single stars, that is, a continuous spectrum, with faint indications of the existence of dark lines or bands.

But when we turn to nebulæ either not resolved into stars, or only resolvable with difficulty, we no longer find this general law to prevail. Some among these objects give a continuous spectrum, and may therefore be regarded as really consisting of multitudes of minute stars; but others give a spectrum entirely unlike any which had heretofore been observed in examining the celestial bodies. When Huggins, in August, 1864, directed his telescope, armed with a spectroscope, to one of these nebulæ, he found, to his great surprise, that instead of a continuous spectrum, he obtained a spectrum of three bright lines of a greenish blue colour, as shown in the frontispiece, spectrum 11. At first he thought the spectroscope was out of order, but finding this not to be the case, he recognised the fact that the cloud in stellar space which he was examining consists of glowing gas. Extending his researches, he found that other nebulæ (including the famous Orion nebula and the Dumb-bell nebula) give the same spectrum of three bright lines; in one or two

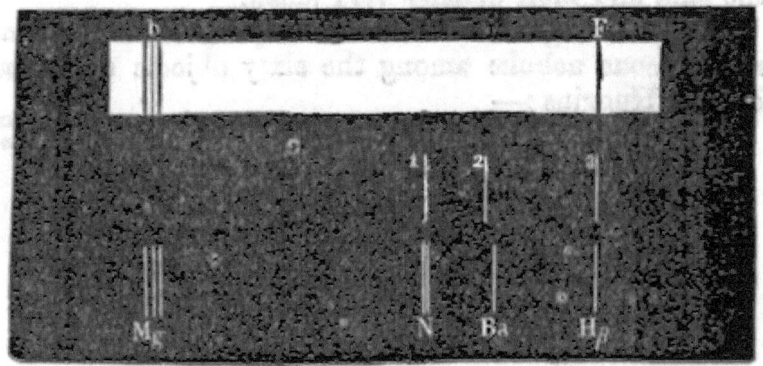

Fig. 61.—Comparison of the spectrum of a gaseous nebula with the lines of certain terrestrial elements.

other cases a fourth line was seen. In order to determine the nature of the gaseous constituents of these nebulæ, he followed the same method which he had applied to the stars. The result is shown in fig. 61. Here the upper spectrum shows the portion of the solar spectrum from the triple *b* line to F; below that are shown the three lines of the gaseous nebulæ, and below that again the triple *b* magnesium line, a double nitrogen line, a line of barium, and the F line of hydrogen. It is seen that the hydrogen line unmistakably agrees in position with the third line of the nebula. The double nitrogen line may be regarded as agreeing with the first line of the nebula, but the middle line (2) of the nebula does not agree with any bright line belonging to thirty elements tried by Huggins, the barium line shown in fig. 61 being near to (2), but not actually coincident with it. As it was shown by Huggins that when the intensity of the light of hydrogen and nitrogen was gradually reduced, the line in each gas coincident with a line of the nebula spectrum was the last to disappear, we may fairly conclude that hydrogen and nitrogen are really present in the gaseous nebulæ. Researches by Frankland and Lockyer on the spectra of hydrogen and nitrogen seem to show that the temperature of the gaseous nebulæ is lower than that of the sun, and their density very small.

The following table indicates the proportion of stellar and gaseous nebulæ among the sixty objects examined by Mr. Huggins:—

	Continuous Spectrum.	Spectrum of Lines.
Clusters	10	0
Resolved, or apparently resolved nebulæ	10	0
Resolvable, or apparently resolvable	5	6
Blue or green, not resolvable	0	4
No resolvability apparent	6	5
	31	15
Not observed through Rosse telescope	10	4
	41	19

COMETS AND METEORS.

It was hoped that the spectroscopic analysis of the light of comets might afford some explanation of the real nature of these strange wanderers. This hope has been but partially fulfilled.

The remarkable comet of 1858, called Donati's, was

examined by Donati himself, and its light was found to give a spectrum consisting of bands; but the principles of spectroscopic analysis not having been established at that time, Donati was not careful to ascertain the exact position of these bands. The great comet of 1861, and the smaller but still important comet of 1862, passed without special spectroscopic examination. At last, in 1866, Tempel's comet, a small telescopic object, was examined by Huggins and Secchi, who found that it gave a faint continuous spectrum, in which Huggins noted one bright band, while Secchi saw three. The inference was that the comet shone in part by its own light (producing the spectral band or bands), and partly, as was to be expected, by reflecting towards us the solar light producing the faint continuous spectrum.

In 1866 and 1867, Huggins observed the spectra of two faint comets with similar results. In 1868, however, two comets of somewhat greater brightness returned, viz., Brorsen's and Winnecke's. As the results of the analysis of these comets were important, it may be well briefly to describe their appearance. Brorsen's (I., 1868) appeared in the telescope like a round nebula, in which the brightness increased rapidly towards the centre; there was a slight extension of the comet in one direction, but no tail properly so called. Winnecke's comet (II., 1868) was just visible to the naked eye. It had a head somewhat resembling Brorsen's comet, and a tail equal in length to about twice the apparent diameter of the moon. The spectrum of Brorsen's comet is shown at 4, fig. 62. The brightest band was the middle one in the green, about midway between b and F; the second was on the left, between b and D; the third was in the indigo. A very faint continuous spectrum formed a sort of background, on which these bands were projected. The spectrum of Winnecke's comet is shown at 3, fig. 62. It consisted of three bands, the brightest in the green, the next bright in the yellow, and the faintest in the blue. All these were best defined on the less refrangible side, and faded off gradually towards the violet.

Huggins compared the spectra of various substances with the spectrum of Winnecke's comet. Amongst others he tried the electric spark in olive oil, obtaining spectrum 1, fig. 62, and in olefiant gas obtaining spectrum 2. The close agreement between the bright

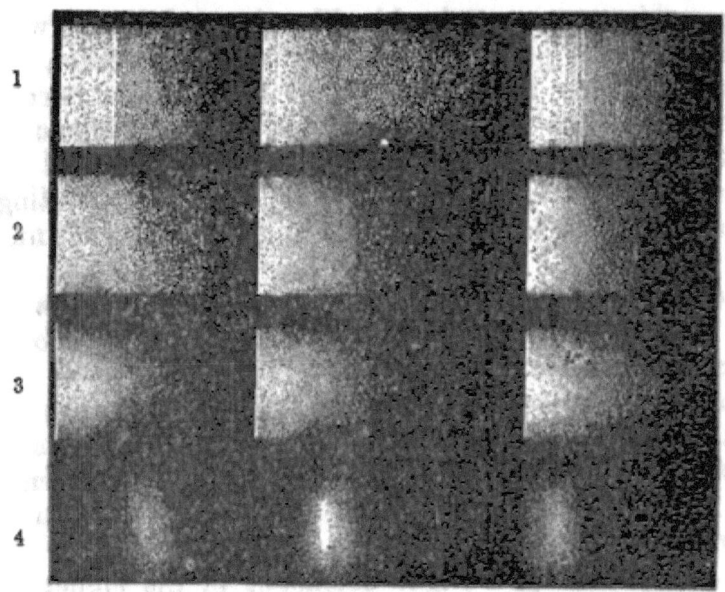

Fig. 62.—Spectra of Brorsen's and Winnecke's comets compared with the spectra of carbon.

bands in these spectra, and those in the spectrum of the comet is obvious. Secchi at Rome, and Wolf at Paris, examined the spectrum of Winnecke's comet with the same general results; Huggins considers that the spectrum of the comet may justly be regarded as that of carbon; but it remains as yet unexplained how so stable a substance as carbon can be present in the form of luminous vapour in the matter of a comet's nucleus. Other comets have since been examined, with results generally similar. The great comet of the year 1874, the only large and long-tailed comet which has been thoroughly analysed with the spectroscope, presented the following interesting phenomena:—"When the slit of the spectroscope was placed across the nucleus and coma, there was seen a broad spectrum, consisting of the same three bands exhibited by comet II., 1868, crossed by a narrow continuous spectrum belonging to the nucleus. On this continuous spectrum Huggins could distinguish no dark lines. There was also a faint broad continuous spectrum on which the three bright bands were projected. When different parts of the comet were examined, the faint continuous spectrum and the bright bands were found to vary in relative brightness. When the slit was shifted from the nucleus to the beginning of the tail, the bands became rapidly fainter, until at a short distance from the nucleus the middle band only could be detected. From these phenomena we may infer that the nucleus of a comet is either solid, liquid, or highly compressed gas, and intensely hot, giving a continuous spectrum; that the coma consists of glowing gas of small density, and at a lower temperature; and that, lastly, the tail consists chiefly of opaque matter which shines by reflecting the solar light.

It has been shown within the past ten years that meteors or falling stars are bodies which travel in flights and streams around the sun, and that some at any rate of these meteoric systems travel in the same track as certain known comets, with which therefore they are presumably associated in some way. The chemical analysis of those larger meteoric masses which have reached the earth shows that they contain iron, nickel, cobalt, copper, tin, chromium, and various silicious compounds. The analysis of meteors has also indicated the presence of oxygen, hydrogen, sulphur, phosphorus, carbon, aluminium, magnesium, calcium, sodium, potassium, manganese, titanium, lead, lithium, and strontium. Those meteors which are dissipated into vapour in the higher regions of the air owing to the intense heat generated by the atmospheric resistance to their rapid motions, have not yet been analysed with the spectroscope. Their light is of course due in part to the intense heat of their solid substance, and not wholly, or even perhaps chiefly, to the glowing vapours into which they are gradually converted while visible (that is to say, while undergoing the process of dissipation).

Certain difficulties present themselves in endeavouring to obtain the spectra of falling stars. These are, chiefly, the suddenness of their appearance, their rapid flight, and the brief continuance of their luminosity. To obviate these difficulties, Browning devised the instrument called the meteor spectroscope, shown in fig. 63. M_1, M_2, and M_3, denote three successive

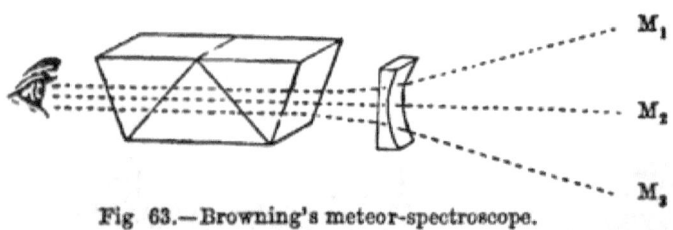

Fig 63.—Browning's meteor-spectroscope.

positions of a meteor; the dotted lines are the paths of rays from M_1, M_2, and M_3 to the concavo-plane cylindric lens. We see that all these rays reach the observer's eye while the instrument is held in the same position. (By placing a double concave lens in front of the cylindric lens, the field of view can be still further increased.) The rays thus received are analysed by the compound direct-vision prism; and owing to the great range of view, the observer will not have to wait long on any night when a star-shower is in progress before a meteor is brought fairly under the action of his meteor-spectroscope. Using this instrument, Mr. Browning, observing in 1866 the meteor-showers of August 10 and November 14, found that the spectra of the heads of meteors are commonly continuous; but in some instances the yellow was so much brighter than the rest as to form a bright band, and in other cases the yellow was almost the only colour visible, though the rest of the spectrum could be just faintly discerned. In two cases the green was the only colour conspicuously visible. The August and the November meteors were alike, or nearly so, as to the spectra of their heads. The tails or tracks of light following the August meteors gave only one yellow line of intense brilliancy, doubtless indicating the presence of glowing sodium. The same had been observed by Professor Alexander Herschel in 1865, who said that in this respect the light of the August meteors resembled that of a spirit-flame largely dosed with salt. The November meteor trains, on the other hand, gave a spectrum continuous over the blue, green, and indigo, very faint in the yellow, and scarcely discernible at all in the orange and red. The yellow line of the August trains was not seen at all in the light of the November meteor trains. Secchi, observing the November meteors in 1868, noticed one, the train of which remained visible for a quarter of an hour. The spectrum of this train consisted of several bright bands in the red, yellow, green, and blue. He was also able by good fortune to analyse two meteors directly, and found the magnesium line (or set of lines) very distinct. Some lines also were visible in the red.

These investigations show that meteors consist of incandescent solid particles, but that these particles are partially dissipated into vapour during the passage of the meteor through our atmosphere. We perceive also that a difference exists between the August and November meteors; and we may well believe that when in future years all the chief meteor systems have been analysed, as well as the comets with which all or most of them will have been associated, important light will be thrown upon the mysterious questions at present connected with meteoric and cometic astronomy.

THE MOON AND PLANETS.

As the moon and planets shine by reflected sunlight, their spectra are the same as the solar spectrum, subject only to such modifications as may be due to the absorptive action of the atmospheric envelopes of these bodies. Thus though we cannot expect to learn anything respecting the substance of the moon or planets from the spectroscopic analysis of their light, we may perhaps be able to ascertain the nature of the vapours which constitute their atmospheres.

All observers of the lunar spectrum agree in stating that it is exactly identical with the solar spectrum. We may infer, then, that whatever atmosphere the moon may possess is too rare to exercise any recognisable absorptive action on the light received through it upon the moon and reflected through it a second time to the observer on the earth.

The spectra of the planets Venus and Mars show the same dark lines as the solar spectrum, but in addition show absorptive bands agreeing in position with the dark bands which make their appearance in the solar spectrum when the sun is near the horizon. These last-named bands, as will be shown in the next chapter, are due to the presence of aqueous vapour in our atmosphere. We may infer, then, that the atmospheres of Venus and Mars contain aqueous vapour, and therefore that there are seas and oceans on the surface of these planets. It is true that, as we analyse the light from these orbs after it has passed through our own atmosphere, doubt might exist whether the aqueous vapour producing the bands in their spectra was in the atmosphere of those planets, or was simply that which is present almost always in our own air. This doubt was disposed of, however, in the case of Mars, by observations made by Mr. Huggins on the same evening— upon Mars when high above the horizon, and upon the moon when lower down; as the bands were visible in the spectrum of Mars and not in the spectrum of the moon, though the moon was shining through a greater range of our own air, it followed that the bands were due to the presence of aqueous vapour beyond our air, and necessarily therefore in the atmosphere of Mars. In the case of Venus, the observations made during the recent transit of Venus effectually disposed of all doubt. On that occasion the light of the sun just before total immersion and just after the planet had begun to emerge, was bent round the body of the planet by the refractive power of the planet's atmosphere. The fine arc of sunlight thus brought into view was analysed by Tacchini, and was found to give a spectrum showing the bands of aqueous vapour. If we remember that it was sunlight received through the planet's air by horizontal refraction (just as we receive sunlight when the sun is really below the horizon but appears raised above it by atmospheric refraction; only that in the case of the planet the sunlight had passed twice through the atmospheric strata), it will be clear that the bands seen in the spectrum of the sun's light so received must have been almost entirely due to the atmosphere of Venus and very little to our own (the sun being high above our horizon at the time). Hence Venus, like Mars, has aqueous vapour in her air, and seas and oceans upon her surface.

According to Huggins the spectrum of Jupiter, besides the solar lines, presents several in the red corresponding to the lines which are seen in the solar spectrum when the sun is low down, and one line which is neither solar nor telluric. The spectrum of Saturn shows some of the telluric lines, and these being less clearly seen in the spectrum of the ring than in that of the globe, it is inferred that the light from the ring suffers less from absorption than the light from Saturn itself. Janssen and Secchi agree that aqueous vapour is present in the atmospheres both of Jupiter and Saturn; and Secchi says that there are lines in the spectrum of Saturn which are not coincident with any known solar telluric lines. It thus appears probable that both Jupiter and

Saturn have gases in their atmosphere which are not present in our own.

A somewhat marked difference exists between the accounts given by Secchi and by Huggins of the spectrum of Uranus. Whereas Secchi asserts the existence of several strongly defined dark bands, and especially of one very broad band in the orange-yellow, Huggins denies that any broad dark bands exist. He asserts that there are six strong lines, one of which agrees in position with the hydrogen F line. Three others of the lines agree in position with the bright lines of our own atmosphere; but there are no bands like those seen in the solar spectrum when the sun is low down. Possibly the discrepancy between Secchi and Huggins may have been caused by real variations in the condition of the atmosphere of Uranus.

Secchi describes the spectrum of Neptune as similar to that of Uranus; but the value of this observation must be regarded as doubtful, until the difference between Secchi and Huggins in the matter of the spectrum of Uranus has been satisfactorily cleared up.

CHAPTER VII.

ATMOSPHERIC LINES IN THE SOLAR SPECTRUM.

WE have seen that some of the dark lines in the solar spectrum become stronger, and that other lines make their appearance, when the sun is low down, and thus shines through a longer range of our atmosphere. In 1860, Brewster and Gladstone re-examined the subject of these presumably atmospheric lines. They drew a picture of the solar spectrum, showing more than 2,000 dark lines, and amongst these they recognised a great number which appear to belong to our atmosphere. Soon after, Professor Cooke, of Cambridge (America), recognised the dependence of many of these lines upon the relative moistness of the air. He found that when the hygrometer indicates moistness, the lines are stronger than when the air is dry. In 1864, Janssen, using a spectroscope with five prisms, succeeded in resolving the dark bands seen by Brewster and Gladstone into fine lines, and ascertained that these lines vary in strength. They are darkest at sunrise and sunset, and weakest (but never entirely absent) at noon. Observing next from the summit of the Faulhorn, about 9,000 feet above the sea-level, he found that these lines were still further reduced in strength. In order to ascertain whether these lines are entirely due to our atmosphere, he caused large pine-fires to be made at Geneva, about thirteen miles from the Faulhorn, and observed the spectrum of the flame. As he found that some of the dark lines were seen which are observed in the spectrum of the setting sun, it was proved that these lines are caused by our own air. To ascertain next what part the aqueous vapour has in producing these lines, he made use of an iron cylinder 118 feet long, placed at his disposal by the Paris Gas Company. After exhausting it of air by forcing steam through it, he filled it with steam, and closed both ends by pieces of strong plate glass. A bright flame (produced by sixteen gas burners) was placed at one end of the cylinder, and analysed by means of a spectroscope placed at the other end. The light, after thus travelling through 118 feet of aqueous vapour, gave a spectrum crossed by groups of dark lines corresponding to those seen in the spectrum of the horizontal sun. Janssen proved, indeed, in this manner, that almost all the lines then seen (called the *telluric lines*, because not belonging to the sun but to our earth) are due to aqueous vapour. To make assurance doubly sure, he extended his observations to the fixed stars, to see if similar lines appear in their spectra. The results of his observations of these spectra accorded well with those he had already obtained.

Ångström, of Upsala, also made careful observations of the atmospheric dark lines in the spectrum. He agrees with Brewster, that all the changes of colour observed as the sun is setting are explained by the spectroscopic indications of atmospheric absorption.

LIGHTNING.

Lightning being an electric discharge taking place on a rather large scale through air, it is to be expected that the spectrum of lightning would present the bright lines seen in the spectrum of the ordinary electric discharge through air. Captain Herschel, observing during a thunderstorm when the flashes were very numerous, found (by the use of one of Browning's miniature spectroscopes) that among many bright lines the blue nitrogen line was most conspicuous. The red line C of hydrogen was also present. A bright continuous spectrum was also visible.

The spectrum of lightning varies, however. Sometimes both the continuous spectrum and the spectrum of lines are very bright; at others the lines can scarcely be seen; while at others, again, the lines only are visible.

Kundt, of Zurich, gives the following as the result of the spectroscopic analysis of more than fifty flashes: "In addition to the spectrum of bright lines, there always appeared a great number of fainter bands, somewhat broader than the lines, and disposed regularly at equal intervals one from another. The spectra of lines consisted of one and sometimes of two lines in the extreme red, a few very bright lines in the green, and some less bright in the blue, besides a still greater number much fainter, most of which, however, were sharply defined. The spectra of different flashes were so far different, that while certain lines were very brilliant in one flash, they were entirely wanting in another, where they were replaced by a set of lines which were invisible in many other flashes. The spectra of bands were also unlike, the coloured bands in some flashes appearing in the blue and violet; in others in the green as well, and occasionally only in the red. In most cases each flash had only one of these spectra. The spectra of lines were usually given by the forked flashes, while sheet lightning yielded the spectra of bands. In only two cases did the same flash first give a bright spectrum of lines very sharply defined, and then suddenly show a spectrum of bands evenly distributed together."

From these results it appears that the spectrum of lightning depends on the degree of heat excited by the discharge. When the heat is great, as in the case of forked lightning, we have the spectrum of lines due to the gases of the air raised to a glowing state by the heat; where the heat is less, as in the case of the brush-discharge from cloud to cloud, or of the glow-discharge, there is a spectrum of bands only.

AURORA BOREALIS.

The spectral analysis of the light given by the Aurora Borealis has not as yet afforded satisfactory information as to the nature or cause of this marvellous and beautiful phenomenon.

According to Ångström, **the auroral arch gives a spectrum of one bright line**, in the yellow-green, between D and E, and a little to the left of the green calcium band (see the fifth spectrum of the frontispiece, where this is shown as the most refrangible calcium band, except one in the violet). Ångström also observed traces of three faint bands reaching nearly to the F line, but these were only seen once. Ångström notes that the zodiacal light gave the same line for a week together in March, 1867; and also that on one very clear night, when the whole heavens appeared phosphorescent, the line was faintly seen in the spectrum from all parts of the sky. This green line is not coincident with any known telluric or solar line. The splendid auroral display of April 15, 1869, was observed by Professor Winlock, of Harvard Observatory, Mass. He found the spectrum to consist of five bright lines, three of which seemed to correspond closely with the bright lines seen in the coronal spectrum during the eclipse of August 7, 1869.* The same aurora was observed by Rayet and Sorel. The spectrum showed very clearly the line seen by Ångström in 1867, and also the atmospheric lines.

The aurora of April 5, 1850, was examined by Schmidt at Lennep, in the Rhenish Provinces. The spectrum consisted of one remarkably bright and broad line on the right of D towards E (Ångström's, no doubt). The same aurora† was observed at Melbourne by Mr. Ellery. Here the brightest line was found to be in the red near C, somewhat towards D; a greenish band or two appeared near the green calcium lines, and a more refrangible faint band seemed resolvable into lines. "The dark segment of the aurora rested on the sea-horizon. Above this was an arch of greenish auroral light, and from a well-defined boundary of this the rose-coloured streamers extended zenithwards. The red line disappeared immediately the spectroscope was directed to any point below this boundary, and only the green lines remained. The loss and re-appearance of the red line was as sharp as possible as the slit passed from the red to the green region.

The aurora of October 25, 1870, presented the rare phenomenon of an auroral crown. Professor Förster,

---

* Winder, in America, states that the aurora when examined by him always showed a bright line close to D, but less refrangible; he saw also a fainter line in the green, and on one occasion a line in the red.

† The same aurora in the sense of occurring simultaneously, and being undoubtedly due to the same cosmical disturbing cause—the seat of disturbance residing probably in the sun. It is hardly necessary to say that an observer at Melbourne could not possibly have above his horizon the same auroral light which was seen by an observer in Europe.

of Berlin, found that the spectrum of this aurora presented only the green-yellow band, and this band was seen even when the spectroscope was turned to parts of the sky which to the naked eye seemed dark. (Dr. Tietjen had noticed the same line in several parts of the sky some weeks before, when no aurora was visible.) Capron, at Guildford, saw a very bright line in the green, when the spectroscope was turned upon the silver-white rays of the aurora, and could perceive the same lines faintly but distinctly in the spectrum of even the darkest parts of the sky. There was also a much fainter line in the red, apparently coincident with the red line of lithium (spectrum 4, frontispiece). An observer at Torquay saw four lines in the red besides the strong line in the green. Zöllner, at Leipsic, using one of Browning's miniature spectroscopes, obtained a spectrum showing several bands in the violet. It must be explained that the width of the bands is due to the fact that to obtain sufficient light the slit was somewhat widely opened. He considers that the broad faint bands shown in the more refrangible part should be regarded, not as spectral bright bands, but as part of the continuous spectrum, broken up by the dark spaces. From observations made after the aurora had disappeared, he satisfied himself that the red line was not coincident in position with bright bands or lines in the spectrum of either hydrogen, nitrogen, oxygen, or carbonic acid. He infers from his observations that if the light of the aurora be really of an electric character, it must belong to matter at a lower temperature than that at which the spectra of gases rendered luminous in a Geissler's tube can possibly be observed.

Neither this nor any other theory of the aurora can be regarded as established, however, by the observations made up to the present time.

CHAPTER VIII.

MEASURING MOTIONS OF RECESSION AND APPROACH.

ONE of the most interesting applications of spectroscopic analysis remains to be considered, viz., its use in measuring rapid motions of recession from, or approach towards, the observer. I have hitherto in these pages spoken of light as if it were some material substance travelling radially from its source. But in reality light travels in a series of waves, which advance in all directions radially from the source of light, the wave-motion, not any material substance, being thus transmitted. It has been shown that the different refrangibility of light of different colours depends on the differences of the light-waves in length,* or, which comes to the same thing, upon the differences in the rate of vibration. Thus, the waves producing red light vibrate less quickly than those producing orange, those producing orange less quickly than those producing yellow, and so on, the waves producing violet light vibrating most quickly of all.

Since the colour of light, then, depends on the number of vibrations which reach the eye in any given time, it follows that if the eye be approaching the source of light, so as to receive more vibrations from light of any given colour than it would have received if at rest, the colour of that light will be altered to a colour corresponding to a part of the spectrum nearer to the violet; and in like manner if the eye be receding from the source of light so as to receive fewer vibrations than it

---

* It must be explained that this term is understood here to correspond to the distance from wave-crest to wave-crest in liquid undulations, and therefore to what is commonly understood by the breadth of rolling waves. In ordinary language, however, the terms length and breadth are not definitely used. People speak of a long roller, or say "a broad wave came rolling in," meaning the same thing. In science, wave-length means the distance between successive points, lines, or surfaces, at the same phase, according as the waves take place along a line, over a surface, or through space of three dimensions.

otherwise would from light of any given colour, the colour of that light will be altered to a colour corresponding to a part of the spectrum nearer to the red. It does not matter whether the eye or the source of light, or both, be in motion; if the two are approaching each other there is a change of apparent colour, the change being towards the violet end of the spectrum; while if the two are receding from each other the change is towards the red end.

Two points, however, must be noticed. First, no change of colour could be perceived except in white light, or in light produced by a combination of many different tints. Take, for instance, the light from a star, and suppose the star to be approaching at such a rate that rays of a given refrangibility are shifted appreciably towards the violet. Then the whole visible spectrum is thus shifted, and a portion at the violet end being shifted beyond the visible limits of the spectrum, is lost. Now, if the red end of the spectrum marked the actual limit of the rays, this being shifted towards the orange, a certain portion of red light would be wanting from the complete spectrum, which would be complete at the violet end, having, as it were, overflowed on that side. Thus the light of the star would be wanting in red rays, and the star would have a somewhat bluish tint. But we have seen (pp. 40—42) that the red end of the visible spectrum does not mark the actual limit on that side; there are rays not producing any effect on the eye, because in reality the wave-lengths are too great. These wave-lengths being diminished like the rest, it follows that a part of the invisible heat rays are rendered visible as light rays, and complete the spectrum at the red end. Hence the entire spectrum is visible as before, and the star's colour remains unaltered. The second point to be noticed is that for any recognisable change to be produced, even in light of a single wave-length, the rate of approach or of recession must be very great indeed. Light travels at the rate of about 185,000 miles per second, and in order that our approach towards or recession from a source of light may effectively increase or diminish the number of vibrations reaching the eye in any given time, the rate of approach or recession must bear an appreciable relation to this enormous velocity. Suppose, for instance, the velocity of approach to be 1,000 miles per second; then the light-waves would pour in with a velocity of 186,000 miles per second: whereas only 185 of them would have reached the eye if there had been no approach, 186 would now reach it. Thus the breadth of each would be diminished in the proportion of 185 to 186. Similarly if we were receding from the source of light with a velocity of 1,000 miles per second, the apparent breadth of each light-wave would be increased in the proportion of 185 to 184. Now the following table indicates the lengths of the wave-lengths corresponding to various colours of the spectrum:—

Colour.	Length of Wave in parts of an Inch.	Number of Waves.
Extreme red	0.0000266	37640
Red	0.0000256	39180
Orange	0.0000240	41610
Yellow	0.0000227	44000
Green	0.0000211	47460
Blue	0.0000196	51110
Indigo	0.0000185	54070
Violet	0.0000174	57490
Extreme violet	0.0000167	59750

So that to cause red light to appear as orange light, a velocity of approach diminishing the length of the wave in the proportion of 240 to 256, or as 15 to 16, would be required, that is, one-fifteenth of the velocity of light; and the enormous velocity above imagined, 1,000 miles per second, is but 1-185th of the velocity of light, or less than a twelfth part of what would be required to change red light into orange. So with other changes. No velocities which probably exist among the celestial bodies would change light of a definite colour to the next colour of the spectral seven, whether towards the red end or the violet. A comet (that of the year 1843) has been known to rush at the rate of more than 300 miles per second round the sun, at the part where the comet approached nearest to him; and this is the greatest velocity which astronomers have yet known of. Since even a velocity thrice as great would not appreciably change the colour of light of a definite wave-length, and since the light of the stars includes all the wave-lengths of the spectrum, it would appear utterly hopeless to endeavour to estimate motions of recession or approach by noting changes in the colour of light.

But although no change of colour could be noted, a change in the entire spectrum might be observed, if the position of the dark lines were carefully examined. The whole spectrum is shifted if the source of light is approaching or receding, and therefore all the dark lines are shifted. Now if we are assured that any dark line in the spectrum of a star belongs to any element, we can compare its position with the corresponding line of that element at rest, and thus possibly detect any motion of recession or of approach on the part of the star.

I believe that the first *published* reference to this possible method of estimating motions of recession or approach came from my pen. In *Fraser's Magazine* for January, 1868, I said, in an article on coloured stars, that the effects of a motion rapid enough to lengthen or shorten the waves of light proceeding from a star would be "to shift the position of the whole spectrum, and this change would be readily detected by a reference to the spectral lines." A few days after, Mr. Huggins wrote to me that he had been engaged for some time in the attempt to recognise such changes; and four months later he communicated to the Royal Society the announcement that by this method he had succeeded in detecting a motion of recession in the case of the star Sirius.* A month earlier than this Secchi

* The account of this discovery in Lockyer's elementary book on the spectroscope is not correct. He states that Mr. Huggins was

had announced that he had observed Sirius by this method without detecting any sign of motion. His spectroscope in fact did not possess sufficient dispersive power.

The instrument employed by Huggins combined the full dispersive power given by two compound direct-vision prisms and three single prisms, two having a refractive angle of sixty degrees, while the third had an angle of forty-five degrees. Having first satisfied himself that the dark line F in the spectrum of Sirius, see frontispiece, spectrum 10 (compared with spectrum 1), really corresponds with the F line of hydrogen, he carefully examined the position of this line in the spec-

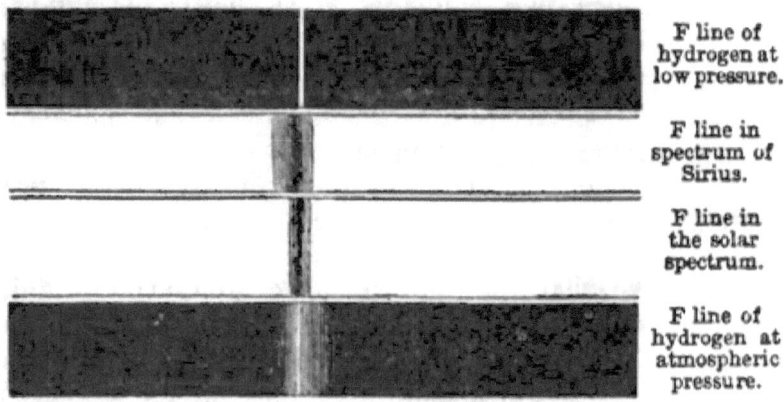

Fig. 64.—Illustrating the displacement of the F line in the spectrum of Sirius.

trum of the star. Fig. 64 illustrates the nature of the displacement he observed. The upper spectrum shows the position of the F line of hydrogen at low pressure;

---

astonished to find the hydrogen lines displaced. This indicates a misapprehension of the exceeding difficulty and delicacy of this method of observation as applied to a star. So far from having his attention directed to the matter by an astonishing displacement of the lines of hydrogen in the spectrum of Sirius, Mr. Huggins had to construct a spectroscope specially to detect the displacement which had escaped both his attention and Dr. Miller's in their careful investigation of the star's spectrum. The figure illustrating the subject in the above-mentioned work is also incorrect.

next is shown the broad F line in the spectrum of Sirius, displaced towards the red. Next is the F line in the solar spectrum. Below that again is the spectrum of hydrogen at atmospheric pressure. It is important to notice these two lower spectra. They indicate what had been observed by Huggins, in confirmation of observations previously made by Plücker and Hittorf, respecting the widening of this line of hydrogen under increase of pressure, viz., that the line widens symmetrically on either side of its position as a thin line. Hence the displacement of the F line of Sirius can be explained only by the motion of Sirius; and as the displacement is towards the red, the star is receding from the earth. The amount of the observed displacement indicated a motion of recession at the rate of about forty-one and a half miles per second. But as the earth had at the time a motion of recession from Sirius, due to her own motion in her orbit, at the rate of about twelve miles per second, there remained a balance of almost twenty-nine and a half miles of recessional motion per second. The sun himself is in motion towards the constellation Hercules, though his rate of motion is uncertain. I place no reliance myself on Otto Struve's estimate of the rate of this motion, having been able to show that the assumptions on which his reasoning is based are not sound. According to his estimate the sun's motion from Sirius would be rather more than three miles per second, leaving about twenty-six miles per second for the actual recession of Sirius from the part of space through which we are travelling. I believe that a much larger proportion of the relative recessional motion of Sirius is due to our sun's motion. Be this as it may, however, there can be no doubt that the distance between Sirius and the sun is increasing at the rate of nearly thirty miles per second; for Huggins's result has since been confirmed by himself with better instrumental means, and also by Mr. Christie at the Greenwich Observatory.

Subsequent observations by Mr. Huggins have

supplied the following indications of stellar motions of recession and approach:—

Stars Receding from the Sun.

Star.	Apparent Motion.	Earth's Motion.	Motion from Sun.
Sirius	26 to 35	−10 to −15	18 to 22
Betelgeux	37	−15	22
Rigel	30	−15	15
Castor	40 to 45	−17	23 to 28
Regulus	30 to 35	−18	12 to 17
β Ursæ Majoris δ ,, ,, ε ,, ,, * γ ,, ,, ζ ,, ,,	60	−9 to −13	17 to 21

Stars Approaching the Sun.

Star.	Apparent Motion.	Earth's Motion.	Motion towards Sun.
Arcturus	50	+ 5	55
Vega	40 to 50	+ 3·9	44 to 54
α Cygni	30	+ 9	39
Pollux	32	+17	49
α Ursæ Majoris	35 to 50	+11	46 to 61

Several of these results have been tested and confirmed by observations made at Greenwich.

The method thus employed upon the stars was

---

* The community of motion of these five stars was a discovery of special interest to me, as I had predicted it more than a year before it was made. My study of the stellar proper motions having indicated the existence of drifting motions among the stars—that is, of cases where groups of stars are travelling onwards together through space—I selected a remarkable case, that of the five stars above bracketed, as one which the spectroscopic method might successfully deal with, all the stars being bright; and in a lecture delivered before the Royal Institution in May, 1870, I expressed my confident belief that all these stars would be found to have a common motion of recession or approach. In May, 1870, I received a letter from Mr. Huggins, stating that these five stars are all receding at a rate of about seventeen miles per second.

manifestly applicable to the sun; and so soon as Huggins's method of observing the prominences without an eclipse had shown that the substance of the prominences often changes in position at the rate of many miles per second, it was natural that observers should endeavour to ascertain whether the prominence matter gave at times spectroscopic evidence of motions of approach or recession. The application of the spectroscopic method is simplified in this case by the fact that the lines for comparison are visible at the same time as the lines affected by the motion. Thus let S S' (fig. 65) represent a portion of a prominence P P' under spectroscopic examination, and let F be the position of the

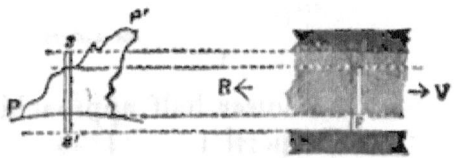

Fig. 65.—Change in the position of prominence F-line due to motion of prominence-matter.

solar dark F-line, while the bright line shown above is the prominent F-line displaced towards the violet. Thus this displacement is recognised. Moreover a higher dispersive power can be used than when the faint spectrum of a star is examined. In the case here illustrated we should know that the prominence matter was moving rapidly towards the observer. This would correspond to the rush of the whole of the prominence matter included within the strip ss' in one direction. Ordinarily we should expect, from what has been seen of the changes affecting the shape of a prominence, to find different parts of the prominence line differently affected. Thus we might meet with such varieties of displacement as are indicated in fig. 66. If the prominence F line appears as at I, we infer that the hydrogen in the part of the solar prominence (or sierra) under examination (that within the strip ss') is approaching the eye, but more rapidly at the upper part, and not at all at the sun's surface S S'. If the F line appeared as at II, we should form a similar inference as to motion of the prominence matter from the eye. If the F line appeared as at III, we should infer that the upper half of the prominence matter was receding

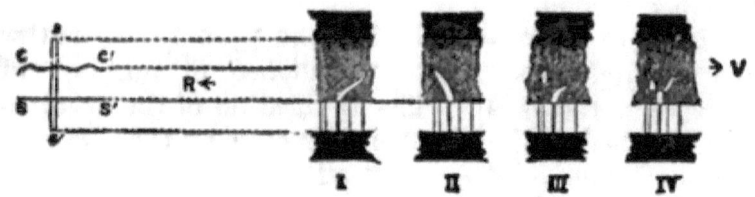

Fig 66 —Spectroscopic indications of rapid movements taking place in the solar atmosphere.

bodily, the lower half approaching, but not so swiftly in its lower portions, and not approaching at all close by the sun's surface. Lastly, if the F line appeared as at IV we should infer that the lower half of the prominence matter was neither approaching nor receding, while the upper part within the range of view was stirred by both kinds of motion, perhaps the nearer portion receding and the remoter approaching, or the remoter receding and the nearer approaching. (The differences of thickness of the F line would indicate varieties of pressure and temperature, as already shown.)

The results of actual observations upon the prominence F line can thus be readily interpreted. The bright F line has been seen as in the first picture of fig. 66, so that the hydrogen matter of the sierra must have been rapidly approaching the observer, the deflection being towards the right, i.e., towards the violet end of the spectrum. This line has been seen as in the second picture when the matter of the sierra was rushing swiftly from the observer. And lastly, when the line was seen bent both ways as in the other pictures of fig. 66, part of the hydrogen of the sierra was rushing swiftly towards, and part was rushing swiftly from, the observer, whence we may infer with considerable probability that a solar cyclone was in progress. In some cases when a prominence-line has been under observation, the spectrum showed a portion of the prominence was neither approaching nor receding from the observer, giving the hydrogen line in its normal position, while a portion was rushing rapidly towards the observer, less swiftly low down, but very rapidly higher up.

There is one circumstance which renders these indications of the approach or recession of prominence or sierra matter somewhat doubtful. Professor Young, of Dartmouth College, has observed that sometimes when the F line of a prominence has shown marked signs of disturbance, the C line has been upright and in its normal position. This is a very perplexing observation, and almost seems to suggest that hydrogen is not in reality an element but compound, the F line belonging to one component, the C line to another, and that the intense heat of the sun separates these two components. There is, however, another and perhaps more satisfactory way of getting over the difficulty, viz., by supposing that under the conditions existing when solar hurricanes are in progress the C line of the hydrogen disappears, so that only the comparatively quiescent portions give both this line and the F line, the disturbed portions giving the latter only.

It is obvious that as the bright hydrogen lines from the prominences or sierra may by their displacement indicate rapid motions of approach or recession, so also the dark hydrogen lines belonging to the ordinary solar spectrum may indicate such motions. In the former case, the motions of approach or recession indicate horizontal motions with respect to the sun's surface; in the latter such motions partake more or less of a vertical character, and where the region observed is near the centre of the solar disc they are almost wholly vertical. But as the ordinary tele-spectroscopic study of the prominences indicate motions both horizontal and vertical with respect to the surface of the sun, we may expect to find spectroscopic indications of both kinds of motion. The displacement of dark lines is indicated in fig. 67.

The narrow strip of the sun's surface under examination (see fig. 44, p. 67) lay across a sun spot, and we see in the appearance of the F line of hydrogen the signs of disturbance in the spot. At the upper and lower extremities this line is of its normal width; then come two parts, one at the top, one at the bottom, where the line is bright, showing the intense heat of the hydrogen at the borders of the spot. Over all the rest of the spectrum's breadth the hydrogen

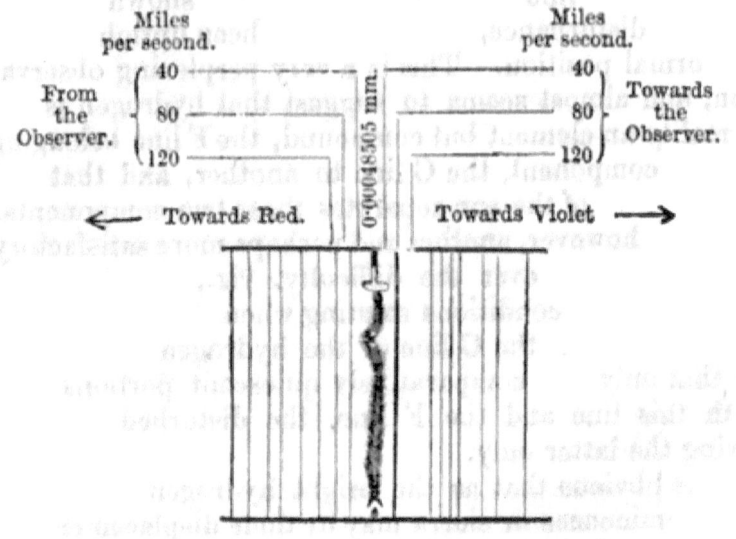

Fig. 67.—Illustrating the spectroscopic evidence of rapid movements in the solar atmosphere.

line is much broader, and is also less defined, than usual. In one place we see it bent towards the red end of the spectrum, indicating a rapid motion of recession, that is to say, the swift down-rush of hydrogen as if into the depths of the spot. The rate of this down-rush is indicated by the numbers placed above (the vertical numerals 0·00048505 mm, indicating the wave-length of light at the place of the F line in millimeters, each equal to a twenty-fifth part of an English inch, very nearly).

The motions which are thus indicated in the vaporous

atmosphere of the sun are so enormous that some evidence other than that derived from the displacement of the spectral lines seems required to confirm results so startling. This therefore seems the place to describe the most striking direct evidence yet obtained of rapid motions in the vaporous matter surrounding the sun.

On September 7th, 1871, Professor Young (then of Dartmouth College, Hanover, N.H., now of Princeton), observed by the spectroscopic method, described at p. 75, the long low-lying cloud of glowing hydrogen, depicted in fig. 68. "It had remained with very little

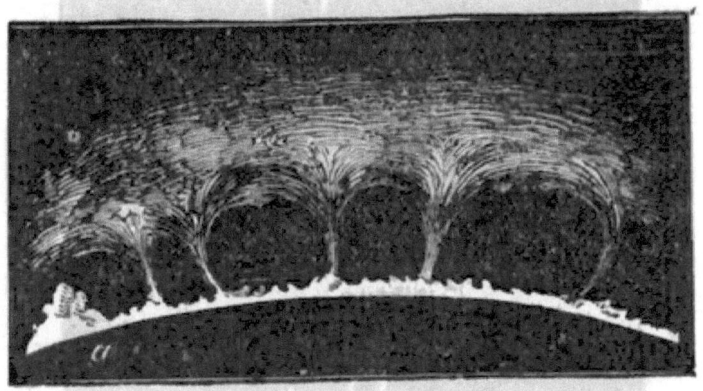

Fig. 68.—Cloud of glowing hydrogen seen by Young, September 7th, 1871, at 12.30.

change," he says, "since the preceding noon—a long, low, quiet-looking cloud, not very dense or brilliant, nor in any way remarkable except for its size. It was made up mostly of filaments nearly horizontal, and floated above the sierra with its lower surface at a height of some 15,000 miles, but was connected with it, as is usually the case, by three or four vertical columns brighter and more active than the rest." . . . In length it measured some 100,000 miles; in height, that is from sun's surface to the uppermost edge of cloud, about 54,000 miles. "At 12.30," proceeds Young, "when I was called away for a few minutes, there was no indication of what was about to happen, except that one of the connecting stems of the southern extremity of the cloud had grown considerably brighter and was curiously bent to one side; and near the base of another at the northern end a little brilliant lump had developed itself, shaped much like a summer thunder-head." Fig. 68 represents the prominence at this time, *a* being the little thunder-head.

"What was my surprise, then," he continues, " on

Fig. 69.—The same prominence region at 1.5 p.m.

returning in less than half an hour (at 12.55), to find that in the meantime the whole thing had been literally blown to shreds by some inconceivable uprush from beneath. In place of the quiet cloud I had left, the air, if I may use the expression, was filled with flying *débris*

—a mass of detached vertical fusiform filaments," each from 4,500 to 13,000 miles long by 900 or 1,300 miles wide, brighter and closer together where the pillars had formerly stood, and rapidly ascending. "When I first looked, some of them had already reached a height of nearly 100,000 miles, and while I watched them they rose with a motion almost perceptible to the eye, until in ten minutes (5 min. past 1) the uppermost were more than 200,000 miles above the solar surface. This was ascertained by careful measurement." The mean of three closely agreeing determinations gave about 207,000 miles as the extreme height attained by these wondrous filaments or wisps of glowing hydrogen, the least of which had a surface largely exceeding that of the British Isles.

The velocity of ascent, more than 100,000 miles in ten minutes, or 166 miles per second, is greater than any velocity hitherto determined by the displacement of lines in the solar spectrum.

Fig. 69 represents the appearance of the hydrogen filaments when some of them had attained the greatest observed height. As the filaments rose, they gradually faded away, and at a quarter-past one only a few filmy wisps, with some brighter streamers low down near the sierra, remained to mark the place. But in the meanwhile the little thunder-head before alluded to had grown and developed wonderfully, into a mass of rolling and ever-changing flame, to speak according to appearances. First it was crowded down, as

Fig. 70 —The same, 1.40 p.m.

it were, along the solar surface; later it rose almost pyramidally 50,000 miles in height; then its summit was drawn out into long filaments and threads which were most curiously rolled backwards and downwards like the volutes of an Ionic capital; and finally it faded

Fig. 71.—The same, 1.55 p.m.

away, and by half-past two had vanished like the other. Figs. 70 and 71 show it in its full development, the former having been sketched at 1h. 40m. and the latter at 1h. 55m. p.m.

The whole prominence suggested most forcibly the idea of an explosion under the great prominence, acting mainly upwards, but also in all directions outwards, and then, after an interval, followed by a corresponding in-rush; and it seems far from impossible that the mysterious coronal streamers, which have now been proved to be truly solar, may find their origin and explanation in such events.

The evidence which this tremendous outburst gave of rapid motions in the solar atmosphere is found to be stronger even, when carefully examined, than it appears on the face of it. I made a calculation at the time when Professor Young's account was first published, as to the circumstances under which matter expelled from the sun would travel upwards to the height observed by Young in this instance—taking ten minutes to pass from a height of 100,000 miles to a height of 200,000 miles— and I found that this could only happen if the expelled matter were resisted (as we should expect) by the atmosphere through which it passed. Expelled with a velocity sufficient just to carry it to a height of 200,000 miles, it would (I found) take much more than ten minutes to traverse the latter half of its upward flight. It must then have been expelled with a much greater velocity, which, being reduced by atmospheric resistance, carried it only to the height to which it would have passed with a smaller initial velocity not reduced by such resistance. The mathematical investigation of the circumstances showed that the initial velocity must have exceeded 300 miles per second, and may have exceeded 500 miles per second. Of course we do not know *certainly* that matter was actually expelled from the sun on that occasion, though it is difficult to suggest any other explanation. The apparent motion of glowing hydrogen may have been due, and indeed very likely was due, not to the actual motion of the hydrogen itself, but to the rush through the hydrogen of a number of missiles (solid or liquid or very dense vapour) flung forth from the sun's interior. These in their swift rush through the hydrogen of the sun's atmosphere would so heat it, by friction, as to cause it to glow with intense brightness. In this case, the glow of the hydrogen filaments would give evidence of the resistance demonstrated by my mathematical investigation of the circumstances of the motion upwards. The filaments themselves would resemble the wisps, looking like streaks of floating matter, often seen after the passage of a large meteoric mass through our own atmosphere.

Similar remarks apply indeed to other cases of the apparent motion of the solar hydrogen. This may be due to the rapid rush through the hydrogen of matter causing it to glow with intense brightness at the place through which the moving matter is at the moment passing.

The whole subject of the spectroscopic evidence of rapid motions of matter towards or from the observer has recently been re-examined, in consequence of doubts thrown out by Secchi and others, who have not only failed to obtain such results as have been described above, but appear to question the mathematical principles on which the method depends. At Greenwich, under the general superintendence of the Astronomer Royal, aided by the great practical experience of Mr. Huggins, this method has been applied afresh to the stars, and also to measure known motions of recession and approach, such as those due to the sun's rotation, to the rotation of Jupiter, to the motion of Venus, and so forth. Secchi had failed to obtain any evidence of the sun's rotation by this method. This is not greatly to be wondered at, seeing that the sun's equatorial parts travel only at the rate of about one mile per second, which though enormous compared with all the forms of motion with which we are familiar, is insignificant compared with those other motions of which this method had barely been able to afford evidence. The Greenwich observers, after being long foiled by the difficulty of the task, have at length succeeded in recognising the sun's rotation spin by the spectroscopic method—no new discovery, it is true, but a veritable triumph of observational skill. It must not be supposed that they simply succeeded in seeing what they knew they ought to see if the method were sound and their instrumental means sufficient. The observations were so conducted that the observer who had to read the spectroscopic evidence had no knowledge of the direction in which it pointed. For the part of the sun under examination was shifted by an assistant observer from one side, where the rotation was bringing the solar surface towards the observer, to the other, where the rotation was carrying it from him, without any intimation of the change. The results were in most satisfactory accordance with theory.

Before the Greenwich observers who earliest took up this task had succeeded in it, Professor Young, with the comparatively feeble power of the Dartmouth College telescope to aid him, but employing a spectroscope of great dispersive power, combining the dispersion of a battery of prisms with that due to the reflexion of light from a closely ruled grating of fine lines,* had succeeded in measuring the rotation of the sun. His results were much more satisfactory, in fact, than those obtained at Greenwich, insomuch that he saw reason for believing that this method may suffice to indicate even the difference of rotation rate between the sun we see and the vapour-strata which produce the absorption lines. Nothing more delicate in spectroscopic research than these observations by Professor Young has probably been ever yet accomplished.

The observers at Greenwich have also succeeded in measuring satisfactorily by this method the rotation of Jupiter, and the motion of Venus in the line of sight. The method when applied to the moon gives, as it should, no evidence of recession or of approach; for the moon has no such motion as this method could measure.

The Greenwich observations of the stars indicate motions of recession and approach agreeing fairly with those determined by Huggins; but as yet much has to be done before any but the most practised spectroscopists can achieve much in the measurement of stellar motions by this extremely delicate and difficult method of observation.

The failure of Secchi and others who have attempted to apply this method must be regarded as due entirely to its difficulty, not, as some among them seem to suppose, to any inherent error in the method itself.

Certainly there has been no more striking or more

* Dr. Rutherfurd, of New York, has succeeded in ruling glass in this way, forming what are called gratings, so closely, that owing to the property called diffraction (in a manner somewhat too complex for explanation in these pages), a spectrum of great purity is formed. A diffraction spectrum thus formed has the advantage over the refraction spectrum of spreading the rays truly according to their wave-length; in fact, it has been by means of such gratings that Ångström has determined the true wave-lengths of light belonging to different parts of the spectrum.

promising application of spectroscopic analysis than this method of determining motions of approach or recession, though it must be admitted that the method is so exceedingly delicate that we cannot at present hope to see it applied to measure any motions save those of enormous rapidity.

ADDENDA.

PHOTOGRAPHS OF STELLAR AND PLANETARY SPECTRA.

Dr. Henry Draper, of New York, and Mr. Huggins, in England, have (almost at the same time) succeeded in photographing the spectra of Vega, Altair, and Sirius, among the fixed stars; of Venus, among the planets; and of the Moon. In the photograph of Vega there are lines (bands or striæ) near the violet end of the spectrum. The photographic spectrum of Venus shows a large number of lines. There is in this spectrum a weakening of the light towards H, and above that line, of the same character which Draper has observed to take place in photographs of the solar spectrum near sunset.

BRIGHT LINE SPECTRA OF NEBULÆ.

Mr. Stone, formerly an assistant at Greenwich Observatory, has communicated to the Royal Society a paper questioning the gaseity of those nebulæ which give a spectrum of bright lines, but on insufficient grounds. He supposes that a *remote* cluster of suns like our own would show the spectrum of the gaseous envelopes of its component stars. But as I pointed out several years since in a paper on the effect of distance on appearance of star clusters, and as Professor Stokes explained after Mr. Stone's paper had been read, distance would not modify the spectrum of a cluster of luminous bodies.

SPECTRUM OF METEORITES.

Mr. Wright, of Yale College, U.S., has found that the gases evolved from meteoric masses, give, at moderate temperature, a spectrum similar to that of Winnecke's Comet, 3, fig. 62, p. 98.

THE TWO FORMS OF COMET SPECTRA.

At Lord Lindsay's Observatory, Dunecht, the spectra of two comets (B & C, 1877) were lately observed, and of these the former gave spectrum 3, fig. 62, p. 98, while the latter gave spectrum 4. The point is interesting, because this is the first observation of the second form of cometic spectra since 1868.

THE END.

ADDENDA.

DISCOVERY OF OXYGEN IN THE SUN.

Dr. H. Draper (see p. 128) has detected the bright lines of Oxygen in photographs of the violet and indigo parts of the solar spectrum. He strongly suspects, also, the presence of bright lines of Nitrogen. What is said at pp. 63 and 64 will indicate the significance of this important discovery so far as its method is concerned, and will show that the fact discovered accords well with what had been before surmised. The concluding sentences of the paragraph on p. 64 illustrate Dr. Draper's inference that the bright background of the solar spectrum is, wholly or partly, made up of the spectra of many gases.

A "NEW STAR" FADING OUT INTO A NEBULA.

The "New Star" described at pp. 92, 93, has gradually faded, the spectrum changing by the gradual disappearance of the continuous or broad-band portions, until in August, 1877 (as seen by Mr. Backhouse), and early in September (as seen by Dr. Copeland, of Lord Lindsay's observatory), only one bright line remained, which had not been the brightest in the original spectrum. This line seems to be identical with the brightest line of the spectrum of the gaseous nebulæ (see pp. 95, 96). The Star has, in fact, faded out into a bluish planetary nebula. Probably the nucleus of such a nebula was the part which acquired unusual lustre, and has since returned to its usual condition. The history of the "New Star" of 1876 no longer accords, therefore, with that of the "New Star" of 1866, as stated at p. 93.

ERRATUM.

On p. 111 line 11, omit the word "except."

www.ingramcontent.com/pod-product-compliance
Lightning Source LLC
Chambersburg PA
CBHW020110170426
43199CB00009B/471